ROMAN
CAVALRY
EQUIPMENT

ROMAN CAVALRY EQUIPMENT

I.P. STEHENSON & K.R. DIXON

TEMPUS

First published 2003

PUBLISHED IN THE UNITED KINGDOM BY:
Tempus Publishing Ltd
The Mill, Brimscombe Port
Stroud, Gloucestershire GL5 2QG

PUBLISHED IN THE UNITED STATES OF AMERICA BY:
Tempus Publishing Inc.
2 Cumberland Street
Charleston, SC 29401

British Library Cataloguing in Publication Data.
A catalogue record for this book is available from the British Library.

ISBN 0 7524 1421 6

Typesetting and origination by Tempus Publishing.
Printed in Great Britain by Midway Colour Print, Wiltshire

CONTENTS

ACKNOWLEDGEMENTS

Firstly, we wish to say a very big thank you to Peter Kemmis Betty, who has been more patient than a very patient thing. Many, many thanks are owed to Susan and to Richard, and to Miriam Daniels for her excellent colour reconstructions. We also wish to thank Philip Clark, Lindsay Allason-Jones, Heinrich Härke, Pat Southern, Jon Coulston, Mike Bishop, Alexandra Croom, Bill Griffiths, Carol van Driel-Murray, Paul Mullis, Ian Pain, Marcus Daniels, Natalie Pollecutt, Sue Rockall, Helen Screene and the staff of Bulmershe Library at the University of Reading, The Museum of the University and the Society of Antiquaries of Newcastle upon Tyne, and The National Tank Museum, Bovington. Please note that all drawings are by K.R. Dixon, with the exception of the colour reconstructions which are by M. Daniels, and illustrations **7**, **12**, **15**, **16**, **17**, **38**, **83** & **94** which are by J.R.A. Underwood.

⊰ 1 ⊱
INTRODUCTION

It is extraordinary what havoc a baker's dozen of horsemen
could inflict on a vast horde of Indians.

J. White, *Cortes and the downfall of the Aztec Empire*

'Well, sir I had known General Custer a long time,' Reno said,
'and I had no confidence in his ability as a soldier.'

E.S. Connell, *Son of the Morning Star*

Cavalrymen as a breed have a reputation for reckless valour and glamorous incompetence. In part this reputation stems from the fact that their successes and failures could be spectacular. For every Le Marchant at Salamanca there is a Ney at Waterloo, and the Romans appear no different; the failure of Julian's cavalry at Strasbourg can be contrasted with the success of Constantine's at the Milvian Bridge.

Yet instances such as these only account for the reckless valour and incompetence. The glamour lay in the cherry coloured overalls of the 11th hussars and the scarlet shakos of the 15th hussars, for as Lactantius noted in the fourth century AD, cavalrymen, particularly those in what would today be considered fashionable regiments, wore extravagant uniforms.

This should not be taken to mean that infantry uniforms were bland in comparison, far from it, although for the cavalryman image, glamour, and a gorgeous uniform were far more important in that they made the cavalryman's job easier. Cavalry were more a psychological, as opposed to a 'sharp pointy', weapon. Their strength lay in their ability to overawe an opponent and then to cut them down as they broke. Indeed, as Napoleon observed, 'In war, morale counts for three quarters, the balance of material force only makes up the remaining quarter'.

This book, although it touches on the mechanics of combat – cavalry did at times have to be sharp and pointy – is concerned with the image of the cavalryman. What the cavalryman looked like, and specifically what the Roman cavalryman from the first to the seventh century AD looked like. In practical terms this breaks down into the following periods – from Augustus to Hadrian, the Antonine period, the third century, the Dominate and the early Byzantine period up until the reign of Heraclius. In the context of this book Byzantine should be taken to mean 'medieval east Roman'.

In defining this image this work is, however, rather partisan, concentrating in the main on unequivocally military items such as helmets, swords etc. and confining grey areas such as clothing and horse harness (with the exception of the saddle) to the colour reconstructions (**colour plates 8, 9, 13 & 16**). The arms and armour under study are arranged by type or class, although the discussion within each chapter is chronological. 'Parade' or 'sports' armour does not warrant a separate section as it is believed that such definitions are not only a modern construct, but also that they are both false and misleading.

The picture constructed is derived wherever possible from a range of contemporary evidence. However, at times our sources (archaeological, literary and representational) are incomplete or to modern eyes opaque, and recourse is taken to comparative and experimental evidence in order to help complete our understanding of the picture. It should thus be borne in mind at all times that when non-contemporary evidence is used the resulting conclusions are 'probabilities or possibilities' rather than actualities.

⚜ 2 ⚜

BEFORE THE PROSAIC

Then from the rampart the Scyldings watchman, whose duty it was to guard the sea-cliffs, saw bright shields carried down the gangway, war-equipment ready for use. Curiosity pricked his mind as to who these men were.

Beowulf, lines 229-33

Before entering the prosaic world of classifications and typologies three other aspects of military equipment studies will be considered. For the evidence, as well as defining the form of an object, can also illuminate, to some extent, the identity of the user at both individual and group level. The reasons behind the adoption of a particular piece or style of equipment and, as will be seen, the function of the more decorative items of military equipment, are areas that are important and will also be examined.

Identity

Soldiers should inscribe their own names as well as those of their centurions upon their shields.

Dio, LXVII.10

At the level of the individual, only the most basic of information can be gleaned. The literate nature of the Roman army, coupled with the personal ownership of equipment by individuals, led to some soldiers tagging, or personally marking their equipment. Thus the names of soldiers and/or the names of the units to which they belonged were at times punched or scratched onto the equipment itself. However, this practice appears to have been by no means universal.

Group identity is at times more elusive. Trends in the distribution of military equipment are certainly discernible. Circular sword chapes, although common in Germany, are rare in Britain. *Felix vtere* belt fittings are in the main a Danubian phenomenon. While Spain has produced its own style of late Roman military dagger, the style in question has also been labeled Hispano-Visigothic.

The distribution of these items may well represent various fashions within army groups and thus by default the army groups themselves. Outliers are explained by the movement of troops around the Empire. Yet it should also be borne in mind that army group, and indeed unit, identity could have been expressed in more perishable and less tangible ways.

Both the British 7th Armoured Brigade (**colour plate 2**) and the German Panzer Group Guderian used painted symbols as identity markers, a jerboa and a capital G respectively. In a Roman context the 'Warrior God' shield from Dura Europos and the images of the eagles and Hercules on the shields on the Arch of Galerius may represent unit badges. It is, however, impossible given paucity of the evidence to say for certain. Equally, styles of clothing, the way for example that belts, cloaks and jewelry were worn, and physical appearance, such as hair styles and facial hair, all conveyed or had the potential to convey the message of group belonging.

Warrior élan

The dress of these ethnic soldiers often comes to represent a particular style of fighting. Hungarians and Poles had long been employed in continental European armies as light cavalry, and their dress came to be associated with the skill and élan with which they carried out that role. Austria had long recruited light cavalry from the hinterlands of her eastern frontier. Hence the members of the Light Brigade, like other many other units of light cavalry in the armies of the industrial world, dressed in a fashion derived from the clothing of the horsemen of eastern Europe.

T.S. Abler, 1999, *Hinterland Warriors and Military Dress*

1 *The Vachères warrior*

The statue of the Vachères warrior (**1**), which dates from the first century BC, is usually described as being that of a Gallic warrior and indeed this may well be the case. However, there is nothing intrinsically wrong in describing the figure as being that of an early Imperial Roman cavalryman. Certainly if you compare the Vachères warrior with a first-century AD Roman cavalry gravestone from Arlon, the similarities – mail shirt with shoulder-doubling, La Tène hilted sword hung from a waist belt, long-sleeved tunic with cuffs – are remarkable.

Whether or not the Roman Republic had a successful cavalry tradition is neither here nor there (although it does appear that they did); what is

13

important is that they had a successful tradition of cultural and technological borrowing.

In the third century BC, most probably as a result of the war against
Pyrrhus, the Roman cavalry equipped itself after the Greek fashion
(Polybius, 6.25.3-11). However, by the first century BC Hellenistic élan
had most definitely faded. It was replaced by the latest dynamic hinterland model. Although it is difficult to assign exact dates, events such as
the routing of 2,000 Moorish horse by a mere 30 Gallic cavalrymen
during Caesar's African campaign (Caesar, *African War*, 6), undoubtedly
led to the adoption in the late Republic of the Celtic four-horned saddle
and the La Tène style long sword.

The expansion of the Empire, and changes in the world beyond the
borders of the Empire, brought the Romans into contact with new, and
at times influential, cultures (**colour plates 4 & 10**). Sarmatian and
Parthian influences account for the adoption of the *contus* in the second
century AD and for changes in helmet design from the Dominate
onwards. Germanic influences affected shield design in the third century
AD. While in the early Byzantine period the Avars had a major impact
on Roman military equipment.

Images of martial terror

The glitter of arms strikes very great fear in the enemy.

Vegetius, *Epitoma Rei Militaris*, II.14

Aside from the practical aspects inherent in the adoption of the dress and
equipment of 'hinterland warriors', there is also the question of the projec-
tion of an image of martial terror. For up until comparatively recently the
battlefield was an arena for display – albeit display with deadly purpose.

Lactantius, in his *Of the Manner in which the Persecutors Died*
(XXXVII), describes the extravagant uniforms worn by Galerius' horse
guard, while Ammianus (XVI.10.8) describes the *cataphracti/clibanarii* of
Constantius, as looking like 'statues polished by the hand of Praxiteles
not men'.

Yet these descriptions should not be dismissed simply as an emperor's whim – this was glamour with purpose. Helmets with tall plumes, brightly painted shields and the flash of metal all combined to help the soldier look and feel more aggressive, to increase his morale and by intimidating the enemy with this peacock display, reduce the enemies morale and make the enemy succumb the easier when battle was joined.

Where then into this picture does the *Hippika Gymnasia* fit? Was it, like 'Buffalo Bill's Wild West' travelling circus, designed to 'wow' provincials and barbarians alike with its mixture of precision and colour? Or should it be viewed, as indeed the Trooping of the Colour is today viewed, as some empty but impressive ceremonial? The answer to both of these questions is no. The Roman army was not given to pointless spectacle, as Titus' pay parade during the Siege of Jerusalem shows.

The answer probably lies in the military (r)evolution of the sixteenth century and to some extent in the Trooping of the Colour, and also by remembering Marcus Aurelius (*Meditations*, VIII.11) and asking 'of each thing, what is it in itself?'

The military revolution, or depending upon your point of view – evolution, of the sixteenth century has been referred to as the 'return of the legions', for the Renaissance-minded reformers of the period did look back to Greek and Roman military treatise for their inspiration. The drill moves created in the sixteenth century, the last flowering of which can be seen at the Trooping of the Colour, were designed to manoeuvre formed bodies of troops in front of the enemy and to deliver a high rate of concentrated fire at an enemy formation. These ideas were, as has been stated, not new – they were taken from Greek and Roman sources – and in this light we should view the *Hippika Gymnasia* not as some abstract display but as a series of battlefield manoeuvres. Indeed the difference between the *caracole* and the *petrinos* is slight.

Nor should we view the highly decorative armour (greaves, helmet) as being reserved solely for the *Hippika Gymnasia*. Returning to Ammianus (XVI.10.8) and his 'statues', a full-face mask helmet was in all probability no different, in terms of the degree of visibility offered to the wearer on the field of battle, to a visored basinet or sallet. Nor was a fully armoured and faceless Roman cavalryman any less effective or impressive than a knight in full late-German Gothic armour (**colour plates 11 & 14**).

❧ 3 ❧
HELMETS

Many of our men fell for the reason that, fighting as they were under the emperor's eye, through the hope of rewards and wishing to be easily recognised they put off their helmets from their heads and so fell victims to the skill of the enemy's archers.

Ammianus XX.II.12

Augustus to Probus

A plethora of cavalry helmets types have been identified from the early and mid-Imperial periods. From the reign of Augustus up until the accession of Diocletian (31 BC-AD 284) Robinson identified 19 types of cavalry helmet – specifically Helmets of the Auxiliary Cavalry A-I and Cavalry Sports Helmets A-J. However, within the trees the wood is discernible and both a general style and indeed a design trend are apparent. Cavalry of the Tiberian period Arch at Orange wear *coolus* type helmets. However, the *coolus* with its flattened, peak-like neck guard was unsuitable as a cavalry helmet, being designed primarily for infantry combat, it left the nape of the riders neck fatally exposed. This situation appears to have been quickly remedied with two main different types the *Weiler* and the *Guisborough* appearing during the first century.

The *Weiler* type (**2**), as typified by examples from Newstead and Xanten, appears to have been confined to the first century. Such helmets were made of iron and covered with an embossed copper-alloy sheathing. Unlike infantry helmets of the period, the cheek-pieces completely covered the wearer's ears. The embossing on the bowl was made to look like hair, whilst the cheek-pieces were decorated with mythological scenes. In order to

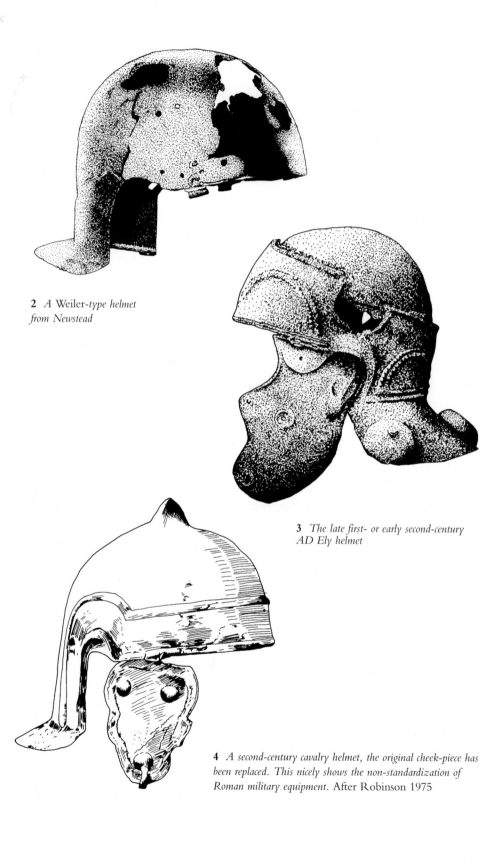

2 *A* Weiler-*type helmet*
from Newstead

3 *The late first- or early second-century*
AD Ely helmet

4 *A second-century cavalry helmet, the original cheek-piece has*
been replaced. This nicely shows the non-standardization of
Roman military equipment. After Robinson 1975

protect the neck, the bowl was extended at the back, down towards the base of the neck and fitted with an angled neck-guard.

The *Guisborough* type is believed to have been introduced in the middle of the first century AD and to have continued in use through into the third. Typified examples from Worthing, Theilenhofen and of course Guisborough are of Attic form. Unlike the *Weiler* type the bowl extended to the base of the neck. *Guisborough*-type helmets had an angled neck-guard, although it was smaller than that seen on *Weiler*-type helmets. Decoration took the form of snakes and mythological scenes, while some, such as the Worthing and Theilenhofen examples had large eagle crests. As with the *Weiler* type the cheek-pieces completely covered the user's ears.

The second and particularly third centuries saw an increase in the level of protection offered by cavalry helmets (**3** & **4**). It also certainly appears to be the case in the third century that similar helmet forms were adopted by both infantry and cavalry units, and indeed it can be argued that this trend continued through into the Late Imperial and Early Byzantine periods.

The new style of helmet is exemplified by examples from Kalkar-Hönnepel (second century), Bodengraven (late second to early third century), Heddernheim (third century) (**5**) and Buch (third century). In general the bowl was either iron or copper-alloy. The bowl extended to the base of the neck where there was an angled neck-guard. On the front of the bowl there was a horizontal or upwardly angled peak. A second-century example from the Waal at Nijmegen has embossed projecting oak and laurel leaves. As with earlier types the cheek-pieces covered the ears; however, they were also extended to overlap on the chin, leaving only a small T-shaped face opening. A common feature, although by no means universal, was the use of crossed reinforcing bars; see for example the helmets from Kalkar-Hönnepel, Friedburg and Heddernheim. The Buch helmet for example had embossed cross-ribs, as opposed to reinforcing bars.

The Antonine period also saw the introduction from the Danubian frontier of conical helmets (**colour plate 8**). These helmets lacked cheek-pieces, but some may well have been fitted with a mail curtain. A conical helmet found near Intercisa may well have been fitted with a mail curtain, while the example from the Dakovo region of the former Yugoslavia probably did not. Conical helmets continued in use through into the third century.

The third-century *Battle of Ebenezer* fresco (**6**) from Dura Europos and the late fourth-, early fifth-century *Vergilius Vaticanus* manuscript (**30**) both

5 *A third-century helmet
from Heddernheim*

show soldiers wearing mail or scale coifs. Unfortunately neither represen-
tation is particularly detailed and it is impossible to say for certain what is
depicted, in constructional terms. Although it is probable that the Dura
Europos fresco shows scale coifs, the *Vergilius Vaticanus* coifs are more likely
to be made from mail. Both materials are of course practicable in construction terms. There is no evidence for the later medieval practice of wearing
a helmet over the coif, however, Maurice (*Strategikon*, I.2) does state that
helmets were worn over hooded coats of mail.

The first century saw the appearance of what are today usually referred
to as 'parade' or 'sports' helmets (**7**). The helmets were made in two parts:
a bowl that covered the top of the head and the neck, and a full-face mask.
Both male and female faces have been found. Male faces tended to be
youthful, with an embossed wavy hair pattern on the bowl. Female helmets
were also decorated with distinctive hairstyles, as well as embossed ribbons,
jewels and diadems. A number of helmets, both male and female, depict

oriental faces. The two halves of the helmet were either hinged together, or, alternatively, a slot at the top of the mask slipped over a hook attached to the underside of the bowl (**8**). In both cases two leather straps, one riveted to each of the lower edges of the mask (one strap had a buckle on the end, which could have been fastened at either the back or the side of the helmet) held the helmet closed. Some full-face helmets, such as a late second-century example from Carnuntum, were fitted with plume tubes on the side of the bowl and loops on the back of the bowl, for ribbons or horsehair streamers. These embellishments were as Arrian (*Ars Tactica*, 34) points out, as much 'a matter of décor as of utility', for they were designed to increase the cavalryman's 'image of martial splendour'.

It would be foolish to ignore Arrian's *Ars Tactica* (**34**) and state that such helmets were not used during the *Hippika Gymnasia;* equally the argument that they were solely used in the *Hippika Gymnasia* is hard to sustain. Arguing that they are too ornate and too restrictive of vision misunderstands both the function of the equipment and the battlefield role of shock cavalry. Whilst Arrian is frequently used to support the *Hippika Gymnasia* argument the fact remains that other authors such as Ammianus (XVI.10.8), Julian (*Orations* I, 37C–38A) and Heliodorus (*Aethiopica*, IX.15) all describe full-face helmets as being pieces of battlefield equipment (**colour plates 11 & 14**). As to their being too ornate, this does rather imply that Roman battle

6 *Mail or scale coifs from the* Battle of Ebenezer *fresco, Dura Europos.* After Kraeling 1956

dress was rather dull and lacking in artistic quality. However, if anything the opposite was true, for if only the archaeological evidence is considered then it is evident that the Roman soldier had a taste for decorated equipment. It is equally apparent that the morale benefits, which accrued from decoration, display and ornament, were both understood and applied by the Roman Army.

In terms of vision restriction, they may well limit the user's field of view. However, no one would consider the medieval visored sallet as being unfit for the battlefield. It is also worth noting that some sallets, such as sallet A82 in the Wallace Collection which was painted to resemble a lion's face, were decorated in order to present a more powerful image of martial terror on the battlefield. Returning to the *Hippika Gymnasia*, such helmets obviously did not impede the cavalryman in the performance of the complex manoeuvres executed in the *Hippika Gymnasia*; why then should they be an impediment on the battlefield?

At this point it must be stressed that although an argument is being advanced for the use of full-face mask helmets beyond a limited role in the

7 *A reconstruction of a Newstead type full-face helmet*

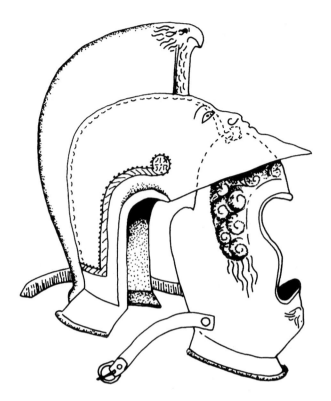

8 *A drawing, based upon a helmet from Heddernheim, showing the hook and slot method attaching the face mask.* After Robinson 1975

9 *A fourth-century 'Intercisa' type 'Ridge' helmet. This example is actually from Intercisa*

Hippika Gymnasia, an argument for a mundane everyday use is not being proposed. Rather what is being proposed is that such helmets were designed for and used in pitched battles and that their use in the *Hippika Gymnasia* was simply battlefield acclimatisation training. A charge by Ammianus' polished statues (XVI.10.8) was undoubtedly a terrifying sight. It is also undoubtedly true these that such helmets did to a degree limit view and were unsuitable for everyday duties such as patrol/reconnaissance and guard duty. Certainly the Antonine period Nawa burial can be used to support this hypothesis. The Nawa burial contained two highly decorated helmets. Helmet A was a full-face mask helmet and was presumably the cavalryman's battle helmet. While the no less decorative helmet B had cavalry cheek-pieces, in that they covered the ear, it was presumably used for other duties such as patrol, reconnaissance, foraging, dispatch riding and guard duty.

Diocletian to Heraclius

The helmet types of the third century disappear in the fourth and are replaced by new styles whose design was heavily influenced by hinterland fashions.

An increase in army size under Diocletian, combined with technological simplicity and a perception of warrior élan lead to the adoption of the Sassanian and Steppe influenced 'Ridge' helmets.

Two types or styles of 'Ridge' helmet were used, a 'simple' or 'Intercisa' type and a more complex or 'Berkasovo' type. It has been argued that 'Intercisa' helmets were infantry helmets and that 'Berkasovo' helmets were cavalry helmets. However, the fact that the cavalry of the fifth-century *Crossing the Red Sea* mosaic from Santa Maria Maggiore, Rome, wear 'Intercisa' type helmets and that the inscription on the 'Berkasovo' type helmet from Deurne shows that the owner of the helmets belonged to the *equites Stablesiani*, points to the fact that both types of 'Ridge' helmet were used by late Roman cavalry units.

'Intercisa' helmet bowls were bipartite, the two halves being connected by a ridged strip (**9** & **10**). The cheek-pieces and neck guards were attached to the helmet's linen or leather lining rather than directly to the bowl itself. Holes pierced around the lower edge of the bowl, around the cheek-pieces and the neck guard, facilitated attachment. Semi-circular or oval cuttings in

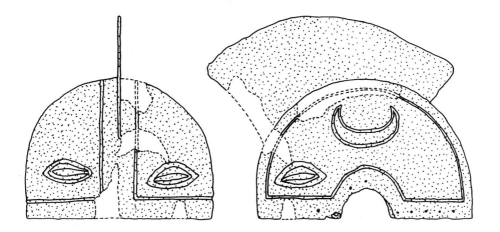

10 *An illustration showing the incised decoration on the helmet in figure* **9**. *This type of decoration can be seen on a number of 'Intercisa' type helmets.* After Klumbach 1973

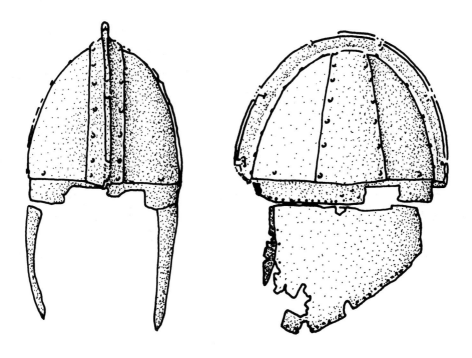

11 *The Concesti helmet*

12 *The Deurne helmet*

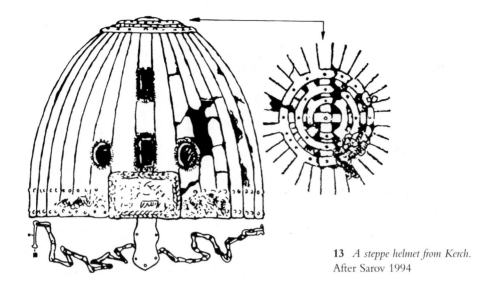

13 *A steppe helmet from Kerch.*
After Sarov 1994

the sides of bowl and in the tops of the cheek-pieces lead to the conclusion that the cheek-pieces were worn over the ears. Traces of silver around the rivets of the surviving examples from Intercisa and Worms, combined with the survival of the silver sheathing from two examples from Augsburg-Pfersee and the fact that some of the 'Intercisa' helmets depicted in Santa Maria Maggiore, Rome, appear to be gold or gilded, points to fact that such helmets were neither as plain nor as boring as their surviving iron components imply.

Interestingly the Augsburg-Pfersee Intercisa's are fitted with a nasal. Nasals, although more a feature of the 'Berkasovo' type, have neither Roman nor Celtic antecedents. Indeed, although known in a European context prior to the Dominate, their last appearance was in the fourth century BC on Greek 'Chalcidian' type helmets. It is highly improbable that the nasal's re-introduction had anything to do what this distant ancestor. Rather, given the fact that nasals appear on both third-centuy Steppe and Sassanian helmets it is more likely that diffusion across the Danubian and Eastern frontiers led to their reappearance after so long an absence.

The gilded silver sheathed helmets from Berkasovo represent the two different bowl forms of the complex 'Ridge' helmet. Berkasovo helmet number 1 (**colour plate 15**) has a bowl divided into four quarters, as do the helmets from Deurne (**12**) and Conceşti (**11**), while Berkasovo helmet number 2 and the Budapest helmet have two part bowls. In all cases an additional band, which curves over each eye, was riveted to the inside of the rim. The T-shaped nasal which was riveted to the front of the helmet, although paralleled by both Steppe and Sassanian finds, was Sassanian in form. The Berkasovo and Deurne helmets also had additional metal bands that masked the joint between the rim and the cheek-pieces. The cheek-pieces, although attached in the same manner as on the 'Intercisa' style helmets, were far larger, covering practically the entire side of the wearer's head and neck. Neck guards had pairs of buckles and were attached via straps, which hung from the inside of the bowl.

The sheathing could be decorated either with a combination of decorating rivet heads and embossed motifs, as was the case with Conceşti, Deurne and Berkasovo 2 helmets. Alternatively, as with the Budapest and Berkasovo I helmets, embossing was combined with glass-paste settings to produce a spectacularly gaudy finish. The embossing appears to derive from Mesopotamian-Iranian helmet tradition and can be seen on a number of

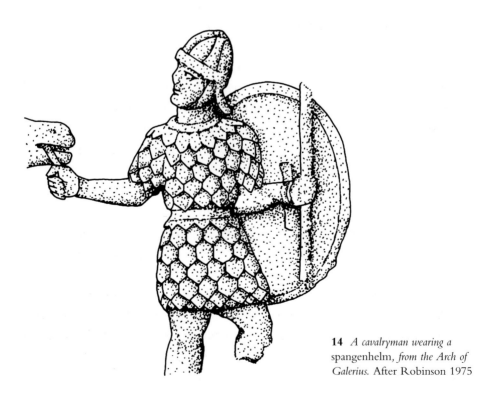

14 *A cavalryman wearing a* spangenhelm, *from the Arch of* Galerius. After Robinson 1975

surviving Parthian and Sassanian helmets and representations of helmets. The glass-paste gems, however, appear rather to be a Steppe innovation; see for example a third-century helmet with glass-paste settings discovered in a horse grave at Kerch in the Crimea (**13**).

Spangenhelme first appear in Roman use on the fourth-century Arch of Galerius (**14**). However, the best evidence for their actual physical form comes from the fifth-sixth-century finds of what are best known as 'Baldenheim' type *spangenhelme*. Strikingly similar in design 'Baldenheim' type helmets were constructed from four or six, at times silvered, iron plates which whilst not touching were nevertheless shaped to form the bowl of the helmet. They overlapped and were attached to the helmet's gilded iron brow band. The brow band curves over the eyes, but unlike the 'Berkasovo' type of helmet, no nasal was attached. The gaps between the iron plates were bridged by four or six *spangen*; inverted T-shaped gilded copper-alloy plates. The helmet was surmounted by a gilded copper-alloy disc with a protruding fungiform button, to which a plume could be attached. Gilded copper-alloy cheek-pieces were, as with the 'Ridge' style of helmet, suspended from the helmets leather or linen lining. The helmets that were decorated with a mixture of classical and Germanic patterns were in all probability made by Roman craftsmen, although their use was not limited to the Roman Army.

Two undated plain iron helmets from Egypt have been used to try and bridge the gap both between second-century *spangenhelme* depictions and the surviving fifth-sixth-century 'Baldenheim' helmets, as well as between the 'Ridge' and 'Baldenheim' styles of helmet. Certainly in the latter case no such bridge need be found as we are dealing with parallel constructional traditions. In the former case too little evidence is undoubtedly being stretched a bit too far. As to the helmets themselves the Der el-Medineh helmet (**15 & 16**) with its 'Berkasovo' type cheek-pieces and T-shaped nasal is probably Roman and probably Tetrarchic in date. It is also probably best viewed as a regional variation rather than as a missing link. The second helmet, the Leiden, was purchased in Thebes in 1828 where it was 'found' on the head of a mummy; it had been placed there by local dealers in order to make the acquisition of both items more attractive. It could be Roman; it could equally date to the ninth century and be of Uighur Turkish origin – a remarkably similar helmet appears on a wall painting from Kumtura in Turkish Central Asia.

15 *A reconstruction of the helmet from Der el-Medineh, as seen from the front*

16 *A reconstruction of the helmet from Der el-Medineh, as seen from the side*

Evidence for the early Byzantine period is, unfortunately, rather limited. The find of a simple 'Intercisa'-type helmet at Kerak, Jordan, shows a degree of continuity with the Dominate, whilst Theophylact Simocatta's (ii.4.3) statement that 'distinctive and conspicuous' helmets were still worn by some Roman troops opens up the possibility that 'Berkasovo' and 'Baldenheim' type helmets were still worn. It is possible that the Byzantine cavalryman depicted on the Isola Rizza dish is wearing a 'Baldenheim' type *spangenhelm*. It is also likely that increasing Avar influence in the sixth century led to the introduction of lamellar helmets such as those found at Niederstotzingen and Kertsch. Maurice (*Strategikon*, I.2) tells us that cavalrymen wore 'helmets with small plumes in the top'; however, such a description could apply to both lamellar helmets and *spangenhelme*.

It is thus probable that the helmet styles which appeared in the Dominate continued in use through into the early Byzantine period and that these styles were supplemented in the sixth century by the appearance of Avar lamellar helmets (**colour plates 11** & **14**).

4

SHIELDS

The names and ranks of soldiers are to be written on the face of their shields. To prevent soldiers straying from their comrades at any time in the confusion of battle, they painted different signs for different cohorts on their shields, digmata as they call them themselves, and it is customary to do this even now. Also the name of each soldier was inscribed in letters on the face of his shield, with a note of which cohort or century he was from.

Vegetius, *Epitoma Rei Militaris*, II.18

To the Imperial Roman Army the shield was an extremely practical piece of equipment. Of course some cavalry units did not use shields, specifically *contus* and bow-armed units of *cataphracti/clibanarii*, *contarii* and *sagittarii* respectively, whilst *dromedarii* may have used a small shield – although this is by no means certain.

For those units which did use it, the shield was primarily a portable obstacle and the first line of defence. But as Vegetius (*Epitoma Rei Militaris*, II.18) points out it was also a display board on which could be read the individual's name, cohort and unit, the designs may also have had an apotropaic significance. From the first up until the mid- to late third century, cavalry shields were either oval, hexagonal or rectangular. Probably the most famous depictions of the oval cavalry shields of the early Imperial period come from Trajan's column. Oval and hexagonal shields are also depicted on a number of first- and second-century AD cavalry tombstones, i.e. those of Titus Flavius Bassus and Vonatorix – oval and hexagonal respectively. Rectangular shields are rarer and are probably best represented by the finds from Doncaster. Taken as a whole the evidence points to the fact that a range of shield shapes existed and that there appeared to be no set rules concerning their use, and the fact of the shield was more important than its shape. However, oval shields predominated. From the late third century onwards hexagonal and rectangular shields continue to be used, although, large circular shields became the predominant form.

Cavalry on the fifth-century *Crossing of the Red Sea* mosaic (Santa Maria Maggiore, Rome) and in the contemporaneous Vatican Virgil are equipped with oval shields, while the later Justinian mosaic, Ravenna (**20**), shows that the oval shield continued in use into the early Byzantine Period. However, increasingly Germanic influence from the third century onwards led to the appearance of both broad oval i.e. the shields from Dura Europos, Syria, and circular shields, i.e. as depicted on the Arches of Galerius and Constantine and on the Piazza Armerina Great Hunt mosaic.

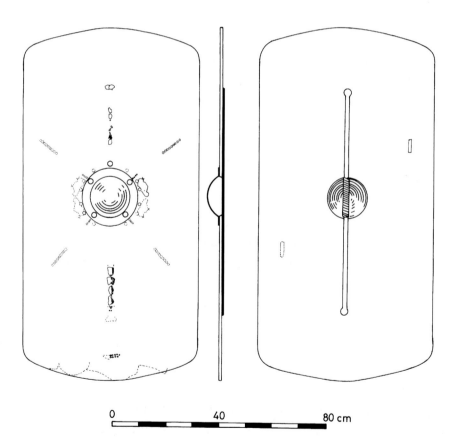

0   40   80 cm

17 *A reconstruction of the external and internal faces of the first-century Doncaster shield. After Buckland 1978*

Young foreigners unskilled with the bow should have lances and shields.

Maurice, *Strategikon*, I.2

At the shoulders, a sort of small shield without a grip, such as to cover the region of the face and neck.

Procopius, *History of the Wars*, I.i.9-15

The shield mentioned by Maurice was probably a normal, centre grip, circular or oval shield. However, Procopius' 'sort of small shield', although undoubtedly made of wood, was not a shield in the conventional sense. Procopius sates that it lacked a grip, it thus probably lacked a boss and would most likely have been strapped in place. Attached to the top of the left arm, it appears to have been a form of what in the late medieval period was referred to as a Grand Guard, and was designed to provide extra protection to the left upper arm, armpit, shoulder and part of the face of a *contus*-armed cavalryman.

In terms of size, the first-/second-century AD leather shield covers from Valkenburg, Netherlands, were between 1-1.5m long, and 52-64cm wide; taking into account the fact that the covers were designed to fold over the edge of the shield, we are then left with shields which were between 7.5-10cm smaller than the size of the cover. While the first-century AD shield from Doncaster was 125cm long and 64cm wide (**17**).

The surviving mid-third-century AD shield boards from Dura Europos ranged in size between 1.07-1.18m in length and 0.92-0.97m in width (**18**). As for the later empire, although no examples survive, extant contemporaneous Germanic shield-board diameter ranged between 0.88-1.10m.

As to the use of small round shields by standard bearers and musicians, this appears to have been a purely infantry phenomenon. The one possible exception to this may have been *Dromedarii* who may well have been equipped, in shield terms, after the Palmyrene fashion – Palmyrene *dromedarii* used a small round shield known as a *cetra* (**colour plate 6**). However, it is equally likely that Roman *dromedarii* used standard Roman cavalry shields. Certainly the fact that they were trained to and expected at times to fight on foot lends weight to the argument that Roman *dromedarii* use normal Roman cavalry shields as opposed to the Palmyrene *cetra* (**colour plate 10**).

From the first to the mid-third century AD the method of construction employed can best be described as plywood, in that the shield board was made from three superimposed layers of wood. Each layer was made up of strips of wood, 30-80mm wide in the case of the Dura Europos plywood shield and 25-50mm (horizontal)/60-100mm (vertical) for the Republican example from Kasr el-Harit. The layers were glued together with the strips on the outer and inner layers running horizontally while those on the middle layer ran vertically. The overall thickness of plywood shields varies from find to find: Dura Europos was 5mm, Doncaster 10mm while Kasr el-Harit was 10mm at the edges and 12mm at the centre. The wood would then be covered front and back with lamb's wool felt, in the case of the Kasr el-Harit shield, or as with the Dura Europos shield, thin leather.

Increasingly Germanic influence in the third century saw the introduction of, for the Romans at least, a new method of shield construction – namely the edge-to-edge glued plank shield. The mid-third-century finds from Dura Europos, Syria contained a number of well-preserved broad

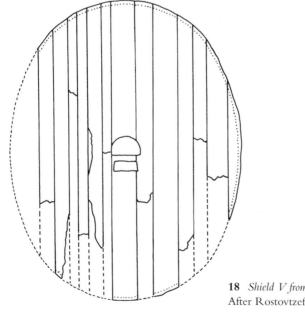

18 *Shield V from Dura Europos.* After Rostovtzeff *et al.* 1939

19 *A highly decorated, third-century, copper-alloy shield boss from Mainz.* After Thomas 1971

20 *A detail of the 'Justinian' Ravenna mosaic*

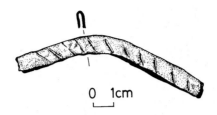

21 *A fragment of copper-alloy shield edge-guttering from Colchester.* After Crummy 1981

0 1cm

oval shield boards. These shieldboards, which measured between 1.07–1.18m in length and 0.92–0.97m in width, were made up of 12–15 poplar wood planks. The planks were between 8–12mm thick and were glued edge to edge.

Archaeological evidence for the construction of Roman shieldboards from the fourth century onwards is sadly lacking. However, the increasing number of Germanic-style circular shields on monuments such as the Arches of Galerius and Constantine and on the Column of Arcadius lends weight to the argument that from the third century onwards plank construction replaced plywood. It is also probable that as with the majority of Germanic shields for the fifth to eighth centuries a leather covering on the front and back of the board was used to increase the shield's stability and thus its effectiveness. The shield was held in the left hand by a single centre grip. Circular and oval hand holes were used on surviving plywood shields, while 'cottage loaf' and 'key hole' shapes are found in the plank shields from the Thorsbjerg bog deposit. The later Viking plank shields from Gokstad had circular hand holes and it is unlikely that this style ever died out. The Dura Europos plank shields had two holes cut for the hand – an upper semicircular one and a lower trapezoidal one; the wood left between the two holes formed part of the grip.

Shield grips, with the exception of the Doncaster shield, which had a vertical grip, were horizontal. The Doncaster shield is also unusual in that the hand hold and thus the grip, although on the central top-bottom axis of the shield, are set above the centre of the shield, being closer to the top of the shield than the bottom. This would alter the shield's balance and tip the bottom of the shield in towards the legs. It has been argued, undoubtedly correctly, that this would make the shield more useful for a cavalryman than an infantryman, as it would help to protect the left leg of the former whilst impeding the latter. It is difficult to say how common this variation was as the rest of the archaeological evidence, and indeed all of the representational evidence, places the boss and thus the grip firmly in the centre of the shield.

The plywood shields from Kasr el-Harit and Dura Europos both have wooden grips, a bone grip was found at Vimose, while the plank shields from Dura Europos were designed to have composite wood/iron grips. Six iron grip-bars were found at Dura Europos; such grip-bars are not unusual and examples are known from the first century onwards. Held in place with disc-headed rivets, they were designed to both strengthen the shield board and to provide a more secure grip. Cloth or leather binding was also undoubtedly used in order to make the grip more comfortable.

Protecting the hand was a shield boss (**19**). Shield bosses in the main were iron; however, copper-alloy examples were also used. The bosses themselves were, in the main, domed with flat circular flanges. A predominately Eastern Empire third-century variant of the domed boss had an eight-pointed as opposed to a round flange. Conical and carinated conical bosses appeared in Pannonia and along the Danubian Frontier in the third century, and this new form continued in use, alongside the more dominant domed form, through into the seventh century. A particularly fine seventh-century Byzantine conical boss, decorated with cast bronze appliqués, was found at Nocera Umbra, Italy.

More pointed bosses, such as that depicted on the Diptych of Stilicho, as well as Germanic-style carinated bosses with pronounced button spikes, typified by the example in inhumation Grave 1/1957 at Liebenau, Germany (**colour plate 12**), appeared in the fourth century and continued in use through into the Byzantine period. The boss was usually attached to the board by four rivets, in a north–south–east–west pattern. In the first and second centuries the rim of the shield was protected by copper-alloy U-sectioned edge-guttering (**21**) which was held in place using copper-alloy rivets inserted through lobate expansions. The lobate expansions were evenly spaced and located opposite each other on either side of the edge-guttering. From the third century onwards, however, rawhide replaced copper-alloy and stitching replaced rivets.

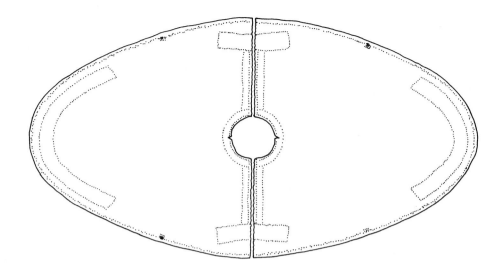

22 *A reconstruction of a cover for an oval shield, from Valkenburg. After Groenman-van Waateringe 1967*

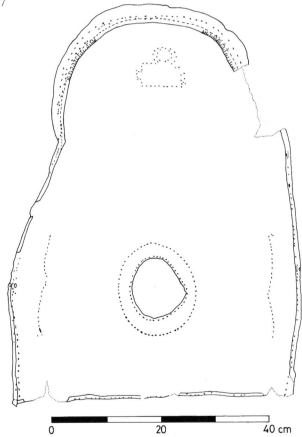

23 *A section of an oval shield cover from Valkenburg. After Groenman-van Waateringe 1987*

0   20   40 cm

Shield covers, designed to protect the shield when not in use, are well attested from the early Imperial Period – see for example the Valkenburg examples (**22** & **23**). Made from goatskin they were fitted with patches that were shaped to cover the boss, and with decorative appliqué panels which contained the unit name or motif. A drawstring around the edge allowed them to be easily and tightly fitted to the shield. A carrying strap, which would have allowed the shield when not in use to be slung either from the saddle (as depicted on Trajan's Column) or on the cavalryman's back, may have been attached to the shield cover. However, it is equally possible, as suggested by the placing of some of the rivets on the Dura Europos plank shields, that any such carrying strap was attached directly to the shield board.

Now the Persians and Alani were discharging their missiles in a practically continuous stream and much faster than their opponents. However, the Roman shields checked the most of them.

Procopius, *History of Wars*, VIII.viii.32-4

The shield was in many ways probably the most effective piece of armour carried by the cavalryman. Those units not equipped with the shield either relied on speed and distance as was the case with the *sagittarii*, or, as with the *cataphracti/clibanarii* and *contarii*, they were compensated by an increase in the level of personal body armour above and beyond that normally worn by the average Roman cavalryman.

As a portable obstacle the shield covered the left-hand side of the cavalryman from shoulder to shin. It was difficult, although not impossible, to penetrate and behind it was a gap which had to be crossed before the body armour was reached.

⊰ 5 ⊱

BODY ARMOUR

Armour for the head, breastplates, and shin guards should be heavy enough to ward off injury but not so heavy as to be burdensome and wear down the strength of the soldiers before they get into action. These should provide protection not only because of their material strength but because of their design and their smoothness, which should cause missiles to glance off and fall to the ground. There should also be a space between the armour and the body. It should not be worn directly over ordinary clothes, as some do to keep down the weight of the armour, but over a garment at least a finger thick.

Anonymous, *Byzantine Treatise on Strategy*, 16

Five types of armour – namely mail, scale, lamellar, solid-scale and composite – were used by the Roman cavalry. Mail, scale and composite armour were in use from the first century, solid-scale appeared in the Antonine Period and was used certainly into the third century and probably into the Dominate. Lamellar is also known from the first century but is more commonly associated with the Early Byzantine Period.

Mail and scale

The Imperial Roman period, from the first up until the later sixth century, probably represented the widest use of metallic body armour in history, with the first and second centuries AD representing a high point of usage within the period as a whole.

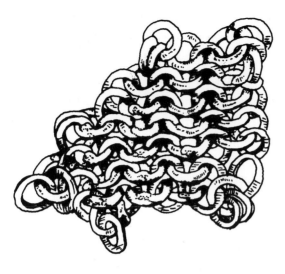

24 *A fragment of copper-alloy mail from 'The Lunt'.* After Hobley 1969

For the Roman cavalryman of the period this armour was predominately mail (*lorica hamata*) (24), although the archaeological record shows, that scale (*lorica squamata*) (26) was also widely used. As to the actual shape of the cuirass, this changed over time; however, both mail and scale adopted the same forms at the same points in time.

In terms of materials, both iron (found at South Shields for example) and copper-alloy (from Grosskrotzenburg) mail shirts are known. At times, as in the case of the third-century Bertoldsheim shirt which had panels of iron mail jointed together by copper-alloy links, the two materials were combined for decorative effect. Copper-alloy (Corbridge, and Newstead), tinned copper-alloy (Ham Hill) and iron scales (Carnuntum) have all been found. A particularly striking effect was achieved by alternating tinned and copper-alloy scales on the same cuirass, see for example the cuirass from Ham Hill.

The cavalry cuirass of the first and second centuries was hip-length, with short side slits. The upper-back, shoulders and chest were given an extra layer of armoured protection, known as shoulder-doubling, which was held in place by a double hook on the chest. The shoulder-doubling also gave the armour a tight protective fit at the neck (25, 27 & **colour plate 9**). Shoulder-doubling disappeared in the Antonine period. It was replaced by a new system of neck closure, which continued in use throughout the third century, namely pairs of small, embossed copper-alloy breastplates. These plates were of two different types. The more common type was made up of two equally sized symmetrical plates that were attached to the armour via rivet holes along their outer edges, and were curved on the upper edge in order to fit around the neck. They were fastened by square headed pins, which passed through slots on each plate and which were themselves held in place by a rod (28). The second form, typified by an example from Bertoldsheim, was made up of two asymmetrical plates (a wide plate and a narrow plate) which together formed a trapezoid. The plates were curved on their upper edge in order to fit around the neck and fastened using a hook and catch-plate mechanism. The centre of the left-hand edge of the main, or wide plate, was extended to form a hook, while a corresponding slot in the narrow plate allowed it to act as a catch-plate.

The third century saw an increase in the area covered by the cuirass. Knee-length armour becomes the norm, see for example the Dura Synagogue frescoes. The change in length, for the cavalryman at least, necessitated the abandonment of the short side slits and the adoption of longer front and back slits. Sleeve length also increased. The short-sleeved cuirasses

25 *A first-century relief from Arlon. Note the shoulder-doubling and the La Tène style sword hilts*

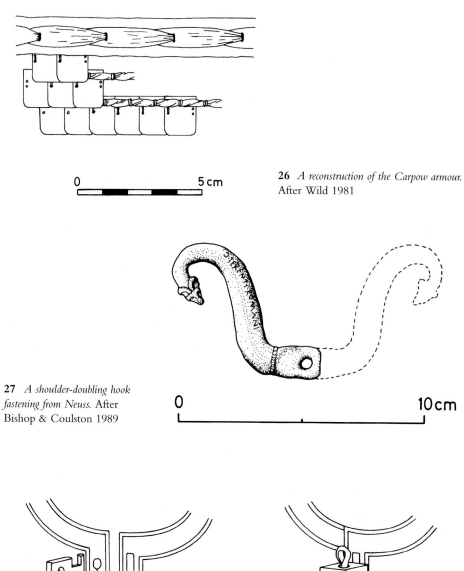

0   5 cm

26 *A reconstruction of the Carpow armour.*
After Wild 1981

27 *A shoulder-doubling hook
fastening from Neuss.* After
Bishop & Coulston 1989

0   10 cm

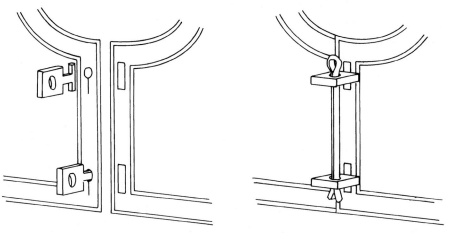

28 *A diagram showing how the symmetrical breastplates fastened.* After Garbsch 1978

of Trajan's Column were replaced by both elbow-length (see for example the relief/tombstone(?) of the armoured soldier from Brigetio) and wrist-length (as shown on the 'Battle of Ebenezer' fresco, Dura Europos) sleeves.

From the representational evidence, it appears that the style of cuirass worn in the third century continued into the fourth, fifth and sixth centuries. A Dominate period Egyptian wood sculpture depicts Roman troops engaged in a siege(?) clad in knee-length, elbow-length mail and scale cuirasses. A painting of a soldier in the Via Latina catacomb, Rome, shows a knee-length, wrist-length mail shirt, while a fragment of relief, which is Tetrarchic in date, and believed to come from the now lost Arch of Diocletian (**31**), depicts two armed soldiers, one in mail and the other in scale. In both cases the armour, on the Arch of Diocletian fragment, has wrist length sleeves and was probably knee-length; the lower legs are unfortunately missing. Neck closure changed again during the Dominate. Archaeologically, breastplates are purely an Antonine and third-century phenomenon. During the Dominate, although we lack archaeological evidence, a number of representational sources do depict the new style. The Egyptian siege(?) wood sculpture in the Museum für Spätantike und Byzantinische Kunst, Berlin, the Santa Maria Maggiore mosaics, Rome, and the Arch of Diocletian(?) fragment in the Vatican Museo Chiarmonti, all show simple wide-necked cuirasses.

In the early Byzantine Period the situation for the most part remains the same as under the Dominate, with Procopius (History of the Wars, I.i.9-15) describing Roman cavalrymen wearing knee-length armour. However, Maurice (*Strategikon*, I.2) (**16**) writing slightly later states that cavalrymen 'should have hooded coats of mail reaching to their ankles'.

Solid-scale

Solid- or semi-rigid scale was essentially an Antonine innovation. Finds from Carnuntum may be pre-Antonine in date; however, the semi-rigid scales from the *Waffenmagazin* were far larger then Antonine examples and may possibly be viewed as an initial stage in the armoured development (**29**).

Antonine and later forms of the armour are typified by finds from Corbridge and Mušov. The scales were small, long and slender, each scale being pierced by four sets of holes. The holes were in vertical pairs, and the

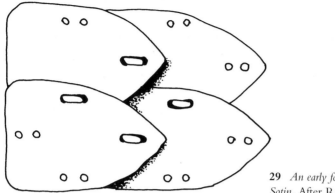

29 *An early form of solid-scale from Sotin.* After Robinson 1975

pairs were placed in a north–south–east–west configuration in the scale. The scales were thus wired not only to their neighbours on each side but also to the scale above and below, forming a (semi-) rigid or solid defence. A tight neck closure was achieved in the Antonine period, and also in the third century, by the use of embossed copper-alloy breastplates.

No complete examples of this form of armour survive; however, experimental reconstructions have shown that it makes an effective form of torso armour. Solid-scale appears to have been employed both on its own and also as an extralayer of torso armour worn over mail in order to provide an increased level of protection against missile and thrusting weapons.

Lamellar

Lamellar was constructed from elongated plates which were laced together to form a rigid defence. The plates themselves could be made from a variety of materials; however, in a Roman context only iron and leather examples are known.

It is also very rare, certainly in the Roman world and it is generally associated with either Steppe influence as in the case of the first-century Čatalka find. Alternatively it was viewed as an Eastern form of armour; indeed the best depiction of it comes from Palmyra, whilst the most impressive Roman finds are the lamellar crinets from Dura Europos.

The rise of Avar influence in the sixth century may well have led to an increase in the use of lamellar by the Roman Army and indeed one of the best depictions of a Roman cavalryman from the early Byzantine period, namely the Isola Rizza dish, is shown wearing lamellar armour (**32** & **colour plate 15**). However, according to Maurice (*Strategikon* 1.2) mail remained the main form of cavalry body armour in this period, although lamellae superseded it in the middle Byzantine period.

Composite armour

Although unusual in a Roman context, composite armour, i.e. where the cuirass is made from more than one type of armour, is not unknown. Fragments of *lorica plumata*, a mail/scale composite, are known from

30 *Mail(?) coifs from the c.AD 400 Vatican Vergil manuscript.* After Coulston 1990

31 *Late third-/early fourth-century depictions of Roman body-armour, possibly from the Arch of Diocletian, Rome.* After Coulston 1990

Augsburg, Ouddorp and Newstead. The Augsburg example which must have looked very splendid when first complete, was made from fine copper-alloy mail covered with alternative iron and copper-alloy scales. The scales themselves were very small, being only 1cm long and 7mm wide.

Probably the most famous depiction of composite armour is the third-century graffito of a *cataphractus/clibanarius* from Dura Europos. The figure appears to be wearing a mail and splint or scale and splint composite armour; however, the crudity of execution makes any definite statement regarding the exact nature on the Dura graffito impossible.

If the Dura Europos graffito is the most famous depiction of Roman composite armour then the most unlikely depiction is from Arlon, France. The relief in question dates to the first century AD and purports to show cavalrymen wearing mail shirts with segmentata shoulder protection. Such an interpretation is, however, in all probability erroneous, and it is far more likely that what is depicted is merely shoulder-doubling.

Padding and effectiveness

So he [Marcellus] charged the Gaul and pierced his breast-plate with his spear.

Plutarch, *Marcellus*, 7

In theory armour is designed to protect the body during combat. In practice, however, the picture was a little more complicated. A number of recent reconstructional experiments, carried out in the Department of Archaeology at the University of Reading, have shown that mail and scale may have been more resilient to penetration than is currently believed.

32 *A Byzantine, lamellar armoured, cavalryman and barbarian opponents from the Isola Rizza dish.* After Menghin n.d.

Indeed those experiments nicely demonstrate the general mitigating effects of armour; in the main fatal blows become wounds and glancing blows become bruises. However, no armour is ever fully proof against the weapons of the enemy. At best(?) it merely delays the inevitable, as in the cases of Sabinus and Julian during the siege of Jerusalem in AD 70 (Josephus, *The Jewish War*, 6.63-6 and 6.85-90 respectively). At worst a blow could be delivered with sufficient force to fatally penetrate the armour. Plutarch (*Marcellus*, 7) describes just such a spear blow, while Ammianus (XVI.12.46), for example, in his account of the Battle of Strasbourg (*Argentoratum*), describes swords cleaving body armour.

Penetration was, however, only half of the problem. For the force of the blow itself could cause damage. The more rigid forms of armour, such as a scale and lamellar, absorbed more of the initial force of the blow than was the case with mail. However, as with penetrative blows no form of armour fully mitigated the effects of blunt trauma. Indeed blunt trauma injuries (broken bones, internal haemorrhaging) which resulted from the force of the blow being transferred through the armour, were just as much of a killer as deep penetrative wounds.

The twin problems of penetrative and blunt trauma were dealt with in two ways. From the third century onwards some classes of troops, specifically close-order infantry and heavy shock cavalry (**colour plates 8, 11 & 14**), increased the number of layers of armour worn by placing a separate piece of torso armour, such as solid-/semi-rigid scale or (possibly as Steppe influence increased) lamellar, over their mail. Caesar's (*Civil War*, III.45) *Scriptores Historiae Augustae* (VI.11), anonymous *De Rebus Bellicis* (XV) and

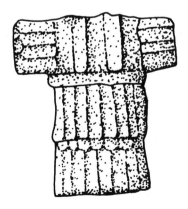

33 *Under-armour padding(?) from the tombstone of Severius Acceptus, Istanbul*

34 *A detail of the statue of the Tetrarchs, Venice: of note are the* pteruges *which would have been attached to a* thoracomachus

an anonymous *Byzantine Treatise on Strategy* (16) all describe the main way in which blunt trauma injuries were reduced, namely by the use of a padded undergarment, which was designed to absorb the force of the blow. The garment, which was known as the *thoracomachus* (*De Rebus Bellicis* XV) or possibly *subarmalis* (*Scriptores Historiae Augustae* VI.11), was worn by all classes of troops in all periods. It was made from wool, felt or possibly linen (*De Rebus Bellicis* XV) and was 'at least a finger thick' (anonymous, *Byzantine Treatise on Strategy*, 16). It was thus in all probability made from two or more layers of cloth stuffed with rags and vertically quilted. In the later empire increasingly heavily armoured troops were matched by the appearance of less armoured, light infantry and cavalry, who it appears dispensed with body-armour yet retained the *thoracomachus* (**33**, **34** & **colour plate 12**).

⚔ 6 ⚔

OTHER ARMOUR

The military man was experienced; he made his spear pass through the younger man's neck; his hand guided it so that he wrenched life from the wicked thief.

The Battle of Maldon, lines 140-43

Throughout the whole of the period under study here, items of armour other than body armour were also worn. Those items were designed to protect, or indeed provide extra protection to those areas of the body, not in the main protected by the cavalryman's body armour.

Three main types of additional armour can be identified: Vambraces or *manica* for the protection of the arms, gorgets for the protection of the neck, and greaves or *ocreae* for the protection of the legs.

Vambraces or *manica*

Segmental or laminated armour arm defences are known archaeologically from a number of sites, most famously Carnuntum and Newstead, but also amongst other places, Richborough, Corbridge, Ulpia Traiana Sarmizegetusa and most recently Carlisle. In representational terms *manica* appear on the early second-century AD Tropaeum Traiani at Adamklissi, the tombstone of Sextus Valerius Severus at Mainz (**35**), as a part of the insignia of the *Magister Officiorum* (Master of Offices) (**36**) in the late fourth to early fifth centuries AD *Notitia Dignitatum,* and on the graffito of the cataphracti from Dura Europos.

35 *The manica from the tombstone of Sextus Valerius Severus, Mainz.* After Simkins 1990

Initially viewed solely as a counter-measure to the Dacian single- and double-handed swords (*falces*) their use now appears to have been more widespread both geographically and temporally. In terms of their cavalry usage they do not appear to have been a piece of general cavalry equipment. The evidence (Ammianus XVI.10.8 and the Dura Graffito) such as it is, points to their use solely by heavy, *contus* armed shock cavalry i.e. *contarii*, *cataphracti/clibanarii*.

In terms of construction both iron (such as the Carnuntum find) and copper-alloy (such as the Newstead find) examples are known. However, the finds are in the main incomplete, although the recently discovered (2001) Carlisle find, containing up to three of these laminated arm guards, (at least one of which appears to be complete), should in the fullness of time − it is currently undergoing conservation − shed more light on the matter.

What evidence there is does allow a partial attempt at reconstruction although there are some unanswerable questions. The Adamklissi Metopes, which can be relied upon as they were in all probability executed by military sculptures, show that the segmental bands overlapped downwards to the wrist. Although it is impossible to say with any certainty given the current level of evidence, it seems likely that they were worn over padding, in which case the Newstead example encased the wearers arm to approximately half of its circumference.

The segmental bands appear to have been attached vertically by leather straps (as was the case with *lorica segmentata*). Holes punched close to the side edges may have been used to secure either an internal lining or under-armour padding.

The exact method of attachment to the arm is currently unknown – lacing, straps or buckles are all possibilities. The degree of flexibility afforded by segmental *manica* is difficult to assess and may indeed have varied between types and over time. The Armenian cataphracts at the battle of Tigranolerta (Artaxata), 69 BC, who are believed to have worn *manicae*, did, according to Plutarch (*Life of Lucullus* 28.3), have their freedom of movement restricted by their armour, whilst the legionaries on the early second-century AD Tropaeum Traiani at Adamklissi appear to have had complete freedom of movement.

Ammianus' (XVI.10.8) description of the *cataphracti* in Constantius' triumph at Rome in AD 357 has been taken to imply that their whole

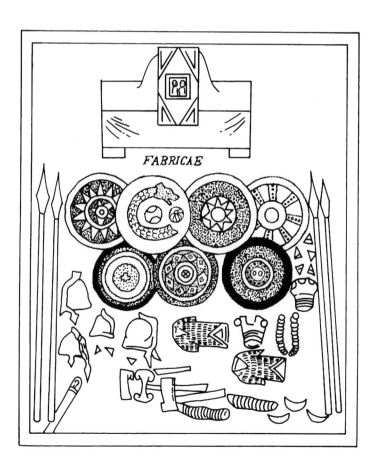

36 *The western* fabricae *(Oc. 9) from the* Notitia Dignitatum. *Note the segmental limb armour*

57

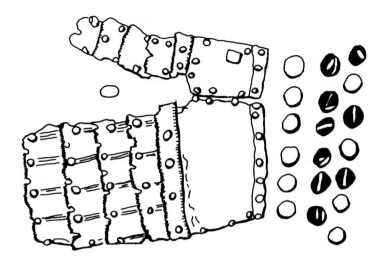

37 *A sixth-/seventh-century iron gauntlet from Iran.* After Nicolle 1993

body, including their hands and feet, were armoured. The evidence for armour for the foot is discussed below in greaves. Evidence for some sort of protection for the hands dates back to the first century AD. The *manica* on the tombstone of Sextus Valerius Severus, at Mainz, has a mitten-shaped end, with one set of bands covering the back of the hand including the fingers, while a separate set of bands protects the thumb. Gauntlets, are also known, albeit in a purely late empire context. The *Strategikon* of Maurice (I.2) recommends the use of iron gauntlets for bucellary troops. A surviving sixth- to seventh-century AD iron gauntlet from Iran (**37**), currently held in the Römische Museum in Mainz, is also mitten shaped and thus has more in common with the tombstone of Sextus Valerius Severus than with later Medieval examples.

Gorgets

> *Since the neck is one of the vital parts, we hold that a covering should be available for it also, standing up from the breastplate itself and shaped to the neck.*

Xenophon, On the Art of Horsemanship, XII.2

As pieces of cavalry equipment gorgets may have been more widely used than *manica*. Xenophon in his fifth-/fourth-century BC work *On the Art of Horsemanship*, saw them as a standard piece of equipment, as indeed did Maurice in his late-sixth/early-seventh century AD *Strategikon* (I.2). However, between these two widely spaced references very few examples exist.

The earliest is a fourth-century BC Macedonian scale gorget from Derveni, Greece, and although it is not as resplendent as the jewelled iron gorget supposedly worn by Alexander at the Battle of Gaugamela, 331 BC (Plutarch *Life of Alexander* 32-3), it is probably the first pertinent, extant, example.

The Derveni gorget was made up of copper-alloy scales backed onto leather, with a pull tie around the top and an opening at the back, where it fastened. A more Roman example, although it may not appear so at first sight, is a second-century AD find from Čatalka in Bulgaria. The Čatalka finds, which apart from the gorget also include, amongst other things a Chinese scabbard slide, full-length splint leg armour, and a Roman full-face cavalry helmet. These beautifully illustrate both the culture and artistic range of equipment available to the Roman soldier.

As for the Čatalka gorget itself (**colour plates 11** & **14**), it consists of an iron ring 0.162m in diameter and 0.07m high. The piece was made in two sections, which were connected by a belt or strap. The outer surface was originally red in colour. Fragments of mail attached to the bottom of the collar suggest that a 'bishop's mantle' or cape type arrangement, in mail, extended the gorget's protection beyond the neck to encompass the top of the chest and shoulders. The third-century AD Brigetio figure (possibly a legionary – there is no inscription) wears a collar which covers both the throat as well as the top of the chest and shoulders. The Brigetio collar covers the normally unarmoured gap between helmet and armour and it is thus believed that this represents a metallic gorget, although the method of construction – scale, mail, or plate – is unknowable, and indeed all of these methods are plausible.

Finally, the *Strategikon* of Maurice (I.2) states that the cavalryman should wear (presumably over his armour) 'round neck pieces of the Avar type made with linen fringes outside and wool inside'.

Certainly padding worn over the armour, as well as under it, is neither an unknown nor unusual phenomenon. However, the exact form of this

38 *H.R. Robinson's reconstruction of a pair of third-century greaves from Straubing*

Avar gorget is open to interpretation as no examples survive, although one may be depicted on a sixth- to eight-century Byzantine manuscript illustration of St Menas (John Rylands Library, MS. S.33).

Greaves

There is a tendency to artificially classify Roman greaves of the early and middle Empire as either field armour or as sports/parade armour. The use of so-called parade armour on the field of battle is discussed at length in chapter two, *Before the Prosaic* and chapter three, *Helmets*; suffice it to say the evidence for purely sports/parade armour is not compelling. The so-called 'field armour' type, as typified by the Künzing example are plain; the latter so-called 'sports/parade' type, of which the finds from the Straubing hoard are possibly the most famous examples, are all highly decorated. However, decorated versions of the 'Künzing' type are known, and plain versions of the 'Straubing' type have also been found (**colour plates 11 & 14**).

The Künzing greaves date to the third century. They were plain iron, 33.5cm long, V-sections with straight flanges on the upper and lower edges and double raised hollows on each side. They were fastened to the leg using leather ties or straps, each greave have four tie-rings, two per side, one at the top and one at the bottom of each side of the greave.

The 'Künzing' style of greaves are usually taken to be infantry greaves, and they do indeed correspond to those worn by legionaries on the Adamklissi metopes; however there is nothing to stop their use by the cavalry.

The Straubing greaves were copper-alloy, and overall, gutter-shaped, although the width changed as you progressed down the leg (**38**). They were the breadth of the leg just below the knee, then widen out over the calf, before narrowing again down to the ankle, they finally widen again over the ankle to form lobate ankle guards. The knee guards, which were hinged, were attached separately and were in all probability fitted after the cavalryman was mounted, as the angle of the knee guard does rather impede movement. They attached to the leg using leather ties or buckles and straps via pairs of opposing tie rings, two pairs on the main body of each greave and one pair on the knee guard.

The quantity and quality of the decoration varies, with both low relief and engraving being used. The decoration itself takes the form of gods and goddesses, both full figures and heads, suckling Romulus and Remus, eagles, dolphins and serpents.

Unlike the 'Künzing'-type greaves the 'Straubing' type greaves would probably only have been used by the cavalry, as the knee guards would have made them unsuitable for use on foot.

The evidence for the use of greaves in the late Imperial/early Byzantine period is literary in nature. Both Vegetius' *Epitoma Rei Militaris* and the anonymous *De Rebus Bellicis* (II.15 and XV respectively) recommend that greaves be worn, but neither source goes into any detail. Procopius (I.i.9.15) states that the cavalryman should be 'fitted out with greaves which extend up to the knee'. While the sixth-century anonymous *Byzantine Treatise on Strategy* (16) states that greaves (along with body armour in general) should be 'heavy enough to ward off injury but not so heavy as to be burdensome and wear down the strength of the soldiers before they get into action. These should provide protection not only because of their material strength but because of their design and smooth-ness, which should cause missiles to glance off and fall to the ground. There should also be a space between the armour and the body. It should not be worn directly over ordinary clothing, as some do to keep down the weight of the armour, but over a garment at least a finger thick.' Finally, Maurice's *Strategikon* (XII.B.4) although describing infantry equipment does say that greaves could be of either iron or more unusually wood. The exact form of such greaves is unknown, the *Strategikon's* statement that wood was used does tend to point towards splint construction, and this is supported by the find of an eight century Turco-Byzantine iron splint greave from Gendjik in the Kuban area. The Gendjik greave, although fragmentary, does fit the earlier literary evidence. The greave would have covered the area from the ankle to the knee, it appeared to have been made up of three broad curved vertical pieces held together by three narrow horizontal bands (one at the top, middle, bottom) – and thus was both splint in construction, yet it presented a smooth glancing surface.

The anonymous *Byzantine Treaty on Strategy* (16) implies that padding was worn under greaves, and although no late examples are known archaeologically, third century AD linen greave linings have been found at Dura Europos, Syria.

The third century AD graffito of the *cataphracti* from Dura Europos shows the rider wearing, what appears to be, full segmental leg and foot armour, and although no finds exist (the Newstead armour is most definitely from the arm) the illustration is supported by Ammianus' (XVI.10.8) description of the *cataphracti* at the Triumph of Constantius who wore

> *. . . thin circles of iron plates, fitted to the curves*
> *of their bodies, completely covered their limbs.*

If no examples of segmental leg armour exist, then the same is not true of splint armour. An early second-century AD grave at Čatalka in Bulgaria contained a set of full-length splint armour for the legs and feet.

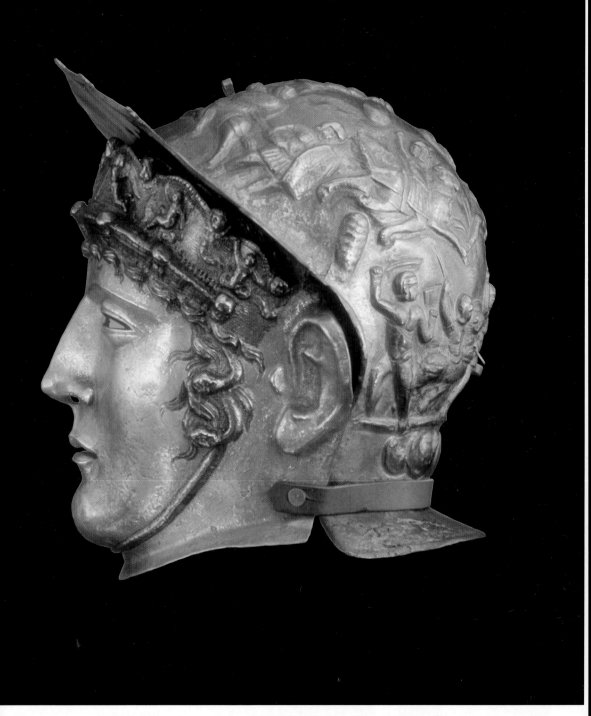

1 *H.R. Robinson's reconstruction of the Ribchester helmet.* Photo C.M. Daniels

2 (above) *The Jerboa of the British 7th Armoured Brigade.* Taken at the National Tank Museum, Bovington

3 (below) *Hinterland Warriors and Military Dress: late second- to mid-third-century Palmyrene dress*

4 (left) *A reconstruction of the Macedonian* sarissa

5 (opposite, top) *A dromedary camel amid the ruins of Palmyra*

6 (opposite, below) *A second- to third-century Palmyrene* dromedarius

7 (opposite) *A reconstruction of an Antonine period cavalryman.* Photo courtesy of W.B. Griffiths

8 (above) *An Antonine period horse archer.* Painted by M. Daniels

9 *Reconstruction: a Flavian cavalryman*. Painted by M. Daniels

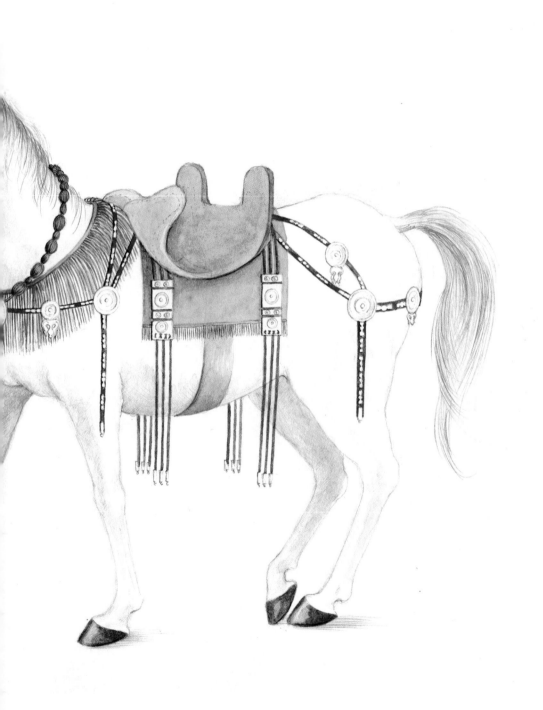

10 *Reconstruction: a third-century dromedarius.* Painted by M. Daniels

11 *Reconstruction: a third-century clibanarius.* Painted by M. Daniels

12 *Reconstruction: a Dominate light cavalryman.* Painted by M. Daniels

13 *Reconstruction: a Typical Tiberio-Claudian harness.* Painted by M. Daniels

14 *Reconstruction: a third century clibanarius.* Painted by M. Daniels

15 *Reconstruction: early Byzantine cavalryman 1.* Painted by M. Daniels

16 *Reconstruction: early Byzantine horse harness.* Painted by M. Daniels

17 *Reconstruction: early Byzantine cavalryman 1.* Painted by M. Daniels

18 *Reconstruction: early Byzantine cavalryman 2.* Painted by M. Daniels

⊰ 7 ⊱

THRUSTING WEAPONS

With bright mail and long swords and spears like a forest

J.R.R. Tolkien, *The Silmarillion.*

These words, although written about a completely different army, nicely describes the majority of Roman cavalry units. For the spear in one form or another was the primary weapon for the majority of Roman cavalrymen over the whole of the period under study. However, before going on to look at the spear in more depth it must first be stated that the term 'lance' will not be used to describe either the cavalry spear or the *contus*, for it is felt that the term 'lance' is confusing and misleading. The word lance primarily conjures up an image of fifteenth-century knights in armour, and although the original knightly lance was indistinguishable from the spear, it is with its later ultimate medieval development that the word is primarily associated. It can be argued that the 'modern' (nineteenth and twentieth century) cavalry lance was similar to the Roman cavalry spear. However, despite any similarities it must be remembered that 'the devil is in the detail' and that both the medieval and modern lance was primarily a weapon designed solely to be used on horseback. Indeed the medieval lance; which was designed to be used couched by a mounted armoured knight against a similarly arrayed opponent; can in many ways be seen as an inflexible technological and tactical dead end. The same cannot be said of the spear.

The spear

Since therefore their arms did not stand the test of experience, they soon took to making them in the Greek fashion, which ensures that the first stroke of the spear-head shall be both well aimed and telling, since the spear is so constructed as to be steady and strong, also that it may continue to be effectively used by reversing it and striking with the spike at the butt end.

Polybius, *The Histories*, VI.25

Spear-armed cavalry predominated in the Roman Army in the period under study. Even in the fifth to seventh centuries AD, the bow did not replace the spear as the cavalryman's primary weapon; rather the bow in the main replaced the javelin as the cavalry's missile capability.

The spear itself was, after the Greek fashion, constructed from a forged, socketed iron head, a wooden shaft and an iron butt-spike. Whilst it remains true that the typological classification of Roman spearheads is fraught with problems, it is, however, possible to divide them into two (three in the late-second to third centuries) groups, namely 'leaf-bladed' (**40** & **41**) and 'angular-bladed' (39). A third group, which was introduced in the Antonine period and continued in use in the third century, had pyramidal blades with either a triangular or square cross-section.

The original Greek butt-spike was a bronze, squared spike, however, by the Imperial Roman period, although retaining its progenitor's stout design; it had become an iron cone (**42**).

Ash was the preferred wood for spear shafts; however, the Romans also used hazel, willow, poplar and alder. In terms of shaft length, although the spear is commonly shown on first and second-century tombstones, such depictions are at best unreliable as the spear has been reduced to fit with the confines imposed by the size of work. Surviving literary descriptions uniformly label it as 'long' and it is only from a few rare surviving archae-ological examples that we can begin to gain an understanding of the uniform, yet subjective, literary description (**43**). A surviving complete spear from the Nydam bog-find has a shaft 10ft in length, while spear-shafts (they lack their heads) from Illerup, vary in length between 7ft and 9ft.

The *Notitia Dignitatum* contains depictions of spear shafts decorated (painted?) with a 'candy-stick/barber pole' pattern. Decorated spear shafts, this time with horizontal bands of colour, are also shown in the hands of soldiers on the early Byzantine Ravenna Justinian mosaic. An alternative form of spear shaft decoration, namely intricately carved interlacing

39 *A third-century, angular-bladed spearhead from Saalburg.* After Jacobi 1897

40 *A third-century, leaf-bladed spearhead from Künzing*

41 *A third-century, leaf-bladed spearhead from Saalburg.* After Jacobi 1897

patterns just below the socket of the spearhead, has been found in the late Imperial period bog deposits at Kragehul. However, it seems that not all spear shafts were decorated from an extant example from Vimose still retains some of the obviously coppiced tree's original bark.

Pennons are usually viewed as a medieval phenomenon, yet they were in use, in a Roman cavalry context, from the sixth century AD. Their use, however, as articulated in the *Strategikon* had more to do with the glitter of arms and the presentation of an image of martial terror, and there is no evidence that they were ever used in battle.

We do not recommend carrying pennons on the spears during battle. For they are as useless in combat as they are valuable for presenting a fine appearance at inspections, sieges, or parades. For whether throwing or stabbing with the spear, the pennon reduces both accuracy and range, and when shooting begins, it interferes with the fire of the archers in the rear ranks. Moreover, in charging, in retreating, in wheeling about, it is no slight inconvenience, and for this reason it should not be used in combat. It is possible, however, to keep both the fine appearance of the battle line at a distance as well as utility. The pennons may be flown until the enemy is about a mile away, then they should be furled and put back into their cases.

Maurice, *Strategikon*, I.10

As to their shape and colour, contemporary sources describe them as *flammula*, a small flame, it thus seems reasonable to infer that they tapered to a point. Colour is, however, more problematic – what colour is a flame? Although it is not possible to give an exact answer it seems likely red, yellow and orange examples existed.

It appears from the *Strategikon* of Maurice that in the early Byzantine period the Avars were the hinterland warriors who dictated military fashion, particularly cavalry fashion. Avar style clothing, saddles, even tents were adopted. While in the case of the spear the Roman's adopted 'cavalry

42 *A reconstruction of a typical iron butt-spike*

43 *A fragment of a late-second/third century relief, possibly a tombstone, from Whitcombe now in Dorchester Museum; note the long spear and round or broad-oval shield*

spears of the Avar type with leather thongs in the middle of the shaft'
(Maurice, *Strategikon*, I.2) (**colour plate 18**). This leather thong has of
course been interpreted as a wrist strap. Such an interpretation is not,
however, supported by the representational evidence, particularly the sixth
century AD Mount Nebo, Jordan, mosaics. According to the *Strategikon*
(XII.D) of Maurice, hunting was a very proper pursuit for the cavalryman.
Its value lay in its ability to simulate the battlefield, for hunting it was
believed, honed both tactical acumen and individual killing skills. Thus the
Mount Nebo, Jordan, old diaconicon-bapistry mosaic, which show two
cavalrymen engaged in this most suitable of military training activity –
namely hunting with long spears – does in all possibility also provide an
accurate portrayal of the use of the spear (as a thrusting weapon) on the
battlefield. In both cases the spear is held, not in the centre, but rather the
spear is held close to the butt-spike thereby maximising the effective length.

A more likely interpretation of the leather thong (*Strategikon*, I.2) is that
it was a carrying loop which allowed the spear to be carried on the right
shoulder (as was indeed the case with nineteenth- and twentieth-century
cavalry lances) when the bow was in use.

First and second-century equestrian tombstones, such as those of Titus Flavius Bassus, Cologne, and Vonatorix, Bonn, and of course Trajan's Column have very much coloured modern understanding of how the spear was used by the cavalryman in the Roman period. However, other representational sources such as the Adamklissi Metopes and the Mount Nebo mosaics show that the Roman cavalryman had at his disposal a range of different techniques.

Used overarm the spear was primarily a missile weapon; although, if held nearer the butt-spike, this method alone allowed a number of downward thrusts all around the horseman onto targets at or near ground level. When used underarm the cavalryman was able to make maximum use of the spear's length and to thrust, with potentially armour piercing lethality, with equal effectiveness against both mounted and unmounted opponents (**46**).

44 *The tombstone of Aduitor. Note the way the rider carries his contus*

45 *A contus armed cavalryman from a Panticapaeum tomb painting*

The *contus*

The *contus*, or *contus Sarmaticus* (Statius, *Achilleid* 131-2) as it is sometimes called, was adopted by the Roman army during the reign of the Emperor Trajan (AD 98-117).

The weapon itself was a very long spear, yet surviving Roman depictions; such as the tombstone of Aduitor, *eques* of *Ala I Caninafatium*, Tipasa, Algeria (**44**), and the riders on the battle of Ebenezer fresco, Dura Europos, Syria; suffer from space constraints and thus do not give an accurate picture of the weapons length. However, comparative evidence, such as the Panticapaeum paintings and the Macedonian cavalry *sarissa*, does allow for an accurate picture of the weapon to be established.

The Panticapaeum, Crimea, tomb paintings (**45**) which date to no later than the mid-second century AD show a number of heavily armoured cavalrymen armed with a long, double-handed spear. The figures are equipped after the Sarmatian style and the spear, probably the *contus*, is at least 4m in length.

The Macedonian cavalry *sarissa* (**colour plate 3**) was in many ways an extremely similar weapon to the *contus*, being a very long spear designed for shock action. Recent research has shown that both cavalry and infantry *sarissa* were identical, in terms of length, namely 12 cubits (Theophrastus,

46 *The ways in which the cavalryman could wield the spear or the contus.* After Nicolle 1980

History of Plants, 3.12.2) or 5.844m. The *sarissa* was potentially a heavy weapon however, the weight appears to have been reduced by the use of both a tapered shaft and a small spearhead.

Thus based upon the comparative evidence it is probable that the *contus* was between 4-6m in length, with a tapering shaft and a small spearhead. From the representational evidence it appears that the *contus* was held in a two-handed underarm grip close to the butt-end of the shaft, either horizontally on the rider's right-hand side, or diagonally across the horse's neck.

In terms of effectiveness, the late third- or early fourth-century AD reliefs at Nash-I Rustam, Iran, show that the weapon was perfectly capable of fatally unseating/overthrowing an armoured opponent.

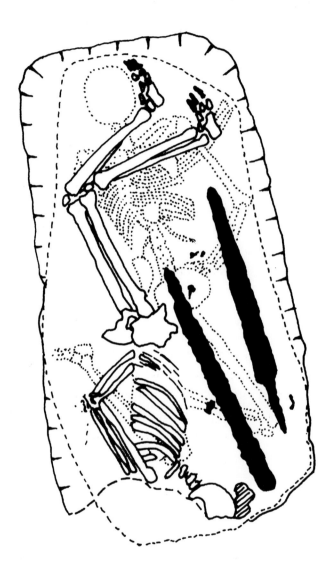

47 *A plan of the Canterbury double inhumation; of particular note are the two long swords.* After Tatton-Brown 1979

⊰ 8 ⊱

BLADED WEAPONS

They had seen wounds caused by arrows, and, rarely, by spears, since they were accustomed to fighting with Greeks and Illyrians; but now they saw bodies dismembered with the 'Spanish' sword, arms cut off with the shoulder attached, or heads severed from bodies, with the necks completely cut through, internal organs exposed, and other horrible wounds, and a general feeling of panic ensued when they discovered the kind of weapons and the kind of men they had to contend with.

Livy, XXXI.34

The Roman cavalryman was expected to fight at close quarters. In order to do so he required a weapon other than the spear, for although the spear is excellent in the initial contact and unrivalled in the pursuit, it is unwieldy in close combat. Thus the imperial cavalryman was equipped with a bladed weapon – primarily the long sword, however the military dagger and axe were also used.

The sword

At some point in the late first century BC the *gladius Hispaniensis* was discarded and replaced by the spatha. The spatha was the Roman version of that design classic, the double-edged long sword (**47**). Based upon Celtic La Tène models the weapon itself remained remarkably unchanged throughout the whole period, although the same cannot be said for hilt and scabbard fittings, both of which changed with the whims of fashion. Sword length over the whole of the period varied between 62cm (24in) and 107cm (42in).

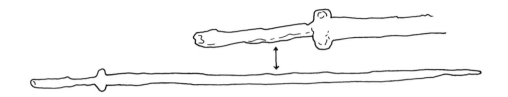

48 *The 1.8m long sword from Aphrodisias.* After Nicolle 1992

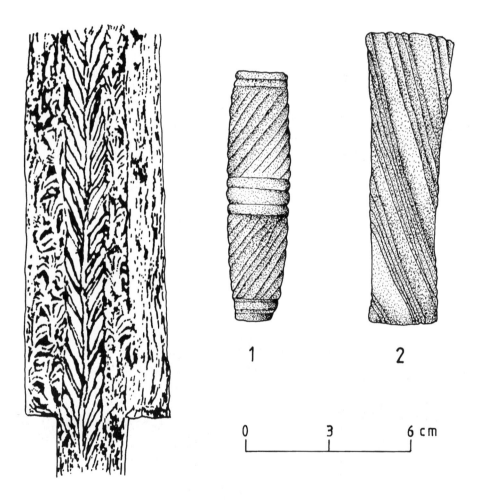

1

2

0   3   6 cm

49 *A detail of the herringbone pattern on a pattern-welded sword blade*

50 *Third-century bone sword grips from Buch (1) and Zugmantel (2).* After Oldenstein 1976

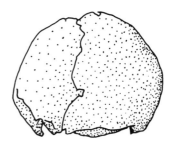

51 *A third-century bone pommel from Zugmantel.*
After Oldenstein 1976

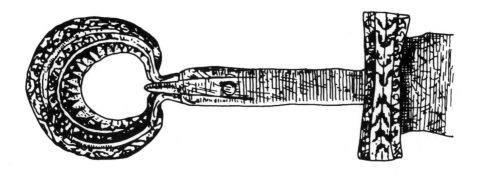

52 *An Antonine period ring-pommel from Poèáply.* After Tejral 1994

53 *A fourth-century decorated silver hilt guard-plate, from Vrasselt*

In the early Imperial period, due to the paucity of finds, no real pattern is discernible – examples from Newstead (length 62.2cm and 63.5cm, width 3.0cm and 3.5cm) are towards the bottom of the range, while an example from Rottweil (length 86.5cm, width 4.4cm) was more in the middle of the range. From the third century onwards, however two distinct types are discernible. The 'Straubing/Nydam' type had long narrow slightly tapering blades. Blade lengths were 68-80cm, whilst blade widths were no greater than 4.4cm. The second type, 'Lauriacum/Hromowka', were shorter and wider, with a parallel-edged blade and a triangular point. Blade lengths for this type were between 55.7–65.5cm, whilst blade widths fell within the range of 6.2-7.5cm. The third century saw the introduction of pattern welded (**49**), fullered (grooved) blades. The fuller gave a deeper backing to the edge without either increasing the weight of the sword or reducing its flexibility. Decorative inlays on the blade start to appear in the third century. These inlays took the form of either a god/goddess (usually Mars, Minerva or Victory), a standard, an eagle or a wreath. It was located at the hilt end of the blade, and was executed in either *orichalcum* (an alloy of zinc and copper) or an other contrasting metal. The inlay, which was undoubtedly apotropaic, was upside down when the sword was in its scabbard, but the correct way up when the sword was in use (**54** & **55**).

In the Early Byzantine Period it is highly probable that longer (length 100-107cm), double-edged, Avar style swords were used by the Roman Cavalry. Straight, single-edged, 'proto-sabres' first appeared in Eastern Europe in the middle-Avar period (c. seventh century AD) and it is likely that they were adopted by some Roman cavalrymen.

Hilt construction was in the main organic, with the guard, grip and pommel being made from either wood, ivory or bone. In the first and second century AD the hilt consisted of a flattened half-ovoid guard, an octagonal-sectioned handgrip and a slightly flattened ovoid pommel.

In the Antonine Period ring-pommel swords with iron guards may well have been used by the cavalry. Surviving examples within the Empire are all short swords, however, contemporaneous long swords with ring-pommels are known from the Bosporan Kingdom (**52**). From the third century onwards guards were either 'arched' (i.e. Butzbach) or rectangular (i.e. Niederbeiber). Grips could be either plain or decorated with ribbing (i.e. Cannstatt), spiral twists (i.e. Zugmantel) or a basket weave design (i.e. Thorsbjerg). Pommels tended to be elliptical in shape, (i.e. Zugmantel or

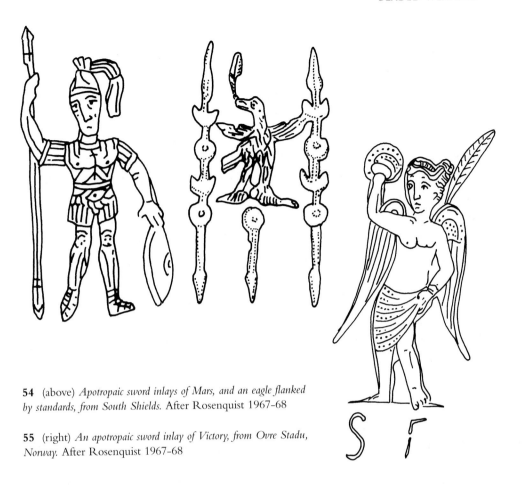

54 (above) *Apotropaic sword inlays of Mars, and an eagle flanked by standards, from South Shields.* After Rosenquist 1967-68

55 (right) *An apotropaic sword inlay of Victory, from Ovre Stadu, Norway.* After Rosenquist 1967-68

Khisfine). Some swords also had a decorated metal guard plate, (such as the fourth century silver example from Vrasselt) which completely covered the bottom of the guard, whilst in the case of a number of the Danish bog finds the guards and pommels were decorated with metal nails (**50, 51 & 53**).

Avar influence in the Early Byzantine Period saw the introduction of a number of difficult hilt designs. The first group had a metal/iron guard and grip, but lacked a pommel (i.e. the sword from Babarc). The second group had a gilded metal guard, a partly gilded metal sheathed grip, and a ring–pommel (i.e. the Szeged-Csengele sword). The third group had a fully gilded metal sheathed grip, but lacked both a guard and a pommel (see for example the sword from Kiszombor). The final group lacked a guard, having only a grip and a small, thin slightly curved pommel (see for example a sword from Visznek) (**73**). Germanic style hilts were also used; one appears

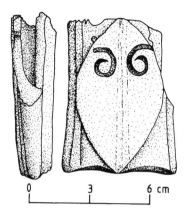

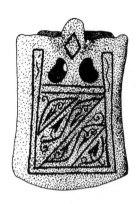

0   3   6 cm

56 *A third-century bone box-chape from Niederbieber.* After Oldenstein 1976

57 *A third-century iron box-chape with niello decoration from Vimose.* After Engelhardt 1869

on the Diptych of Stilicho and the *Strategikon* of Maurice (XII. B.4) speaks of the adoption of Herulian swords, albeit in an infantry context.

Scabbards in the main were made from pairs of leather covered wood plates, although uncovered wooden scabbards are known from a number of Danish bog deposits, namely Kragehul, Nydam and Vimose.

In the first century, triangular guttering chapes were used. This style continued through the second century, although new styles such as heart, peltiform (i.e. the Canterbury and Lyon finds respectively) and semicircular (see the Marcus Column) do appear in the Antonine period (**62**).

From the third century onwards triangular chapes cease to be used. Peltate chapes, however, continue in use throughout the third and into the fourth centuries. The third century also saw the introduction of box and circular chapes (**56, 57** & **58**). Although both of these new styles continued through into the late Imperial period, box chapes appear to have been a European fashion, whereas circular chapes were used, (with the exception of Britain), throughout the Empire.

The statue of the Tetrarchs in Venice depicts a style of chape, which was introduced during the fourth century. This new style or type, typified by examples from Gundremmingen and Liebenau, consisted of an elliptical copper-alloy plate, fitted with three decorative studs (**59, 60** & **61**). Surviving Avar scabbards (such as the finds from Szeged-Csengele and Kiszombor) have cylindrical chapes.

Sword suspension changed a great deal between the first and seventh centuries. The reasons behind the changes were not practical. There was

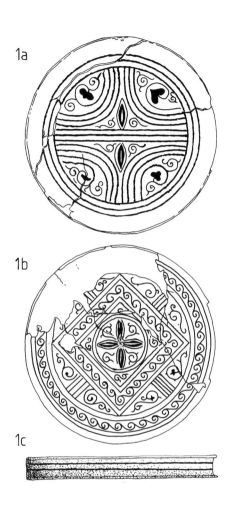

1a

1b

1c

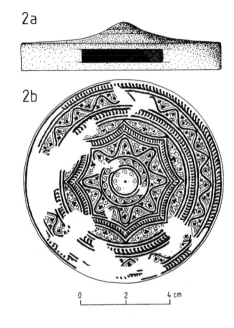

2a

2b

58 *Niello decorated, circular iron chapes from Nydam (1a-c) and Reichersdorf (2a-b).* After Hundt 1953

0   2   4 cm

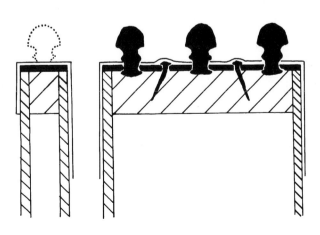

59 *The Dominate period scabbard from Liebenau. The detail shows how the chape was attached to the scabbard.* After Werner 1966

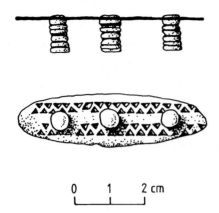

0   1   2 cm

60 *The Dominate period chape from Gundremmingen.* After Werner 1966

nothing intrinsically wrong with any of the methods of sword suspension employed by the Roman cavalry. Nor can it be reasonably argued that one method was superior. As to the reasons behind the changes they undoubtedly lie in the impact of hinterland warrior cultures on the Roman Army and a perceived need to emulate warrior élan via the medium of dress.

Sword suspension in the first and second centuries, up until the end of the Reign of the Emperor Hadrian (AD 117-138), was via a ring suspension system. The decorated locket plates at the top of the scabbard had four suspension rings, two per side. These rings were used to suspend the scabbard, on the right-hand side of the body, either from a plain waist-belt, as can be seen on the tombstones of Romanius, in Mainz and Vonatorix, Bonn (**63**). The scabbard on the tombstone of Romanius also appears to have edge guttering running along the whole of it length. Alternatively a narrow baldric, as can be seen on Trajan's Column, which did not require any form of fastening, was used. As to the number of suspension rings employed, it is uncertain (in both the case of the waist-belt and the baldric) whether two, three or all four were used. Indeed it may be that exact number employed was a matter of individual or unit taste.

In the Antonine period the swords in the main were still worn on the right-hand side. However, the scabbard slide, a steppe invention, replaced ring suspension. It also appears that the sword belt went out of use and the sword was worn exclusively on a narrow baldric.

Scabbard-slides in the second to third centuries were either copper-alloy, iron, bone or ivory. However, a jade Chinese example dating to the second century has been found in a cavalryman's grave at Čatalka in Bulgaria. The metal examples had two or three projecting studs, which would have allowed them to be keyed into the scabbard. In all cases, however, a combination of glue and binding (cloth on leather) would have secured the scabbard slide to the outer face of the scabbard.

Ivory and bone slides were either flat and waisted or raised and lobate. Iron examples were long thin and triangular; decoration was confided to the upper face and consisted of a niello inlay. An iron dolphin slide was found in a grave at Stuttgart-Bad Cannstatt, Germany. Copper-alloy slides were cast either as elongated dolphins, alternatively they were cast with

61 *Two of the swords from the statue of the Tetrarchs, Venice; of note are the chapes and waisted scabbard slides*

decorative ribs, fluting and terminals. The terminals could be either heart shaped, foliate, crescents, rings or peltate (**69, 70, 71 & 72**).

In the third century the sword moved permanently to the left-hand side of the body, gone too was the narrow, fitting-less baldric of earlier centuries. In its place a broad baldric with a tapering end and a circular *phalera* was worn. Surviving baldrics from the bog deposits of Vimose and Thorsbjerg vary in width between 7-9.1cm (tapering to 1.2 at the narrow end) and in length between 1.055m-1.185m (**64 & 65**). They worked by having the broad end with the *phalera*, resting on the right shoulder, and running diagonally across the front of the body. The tapering end went over the back with the narrow end passing twice around the scabbard (through the scabbard slide) in order to tilt the hilt forwards – as is indeed shown on Sassanian depictions of Roman soldiers. The narrow end then passed through the eye of the *phalera* and was sewn in place. The *phalerae* themselves could be either plain or decorated. The decoration took the form of either concentric circles, perforated geometric patterns, raised radiating petals or cast openwork designs. The cast openwork examples varied from the simple-swastikas, radiating hearts, peltae or Celtic designs. To the more elaborate, including a suckling Romulus and Remus from Egypt and an eagle clutching thunderbolts and surrounded by the motto 'OPTIME MAXIME CON[SERVA], examples of which survive from both Britain and Germany (**66 & 67**).

As well as decoration on the *phalera*, the baldric itself could also be decorated. The Vimose finds were decorated with dolphin and foliate designs stitched into the leather. A number of copper-alloy rectangular plates with hinged heart-shaped terminals have also been found, which correspond to the ivory-leaf baldric terminals depicted on a number of third-century tombstones (**68**).

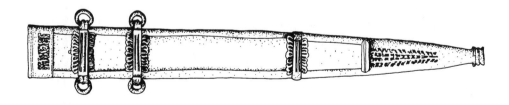

62 *A first-century AD scabbard from the Rhine at Mainz.* After Bishop & Coulston 1993

VONATORIXDV
CONISFEQVESALA
LONGINIANAAN
NORVM·XLV·STIPEN
DIORVM·XVII·H·S·E

63 *The first-century AD tombstone of Vonatorix, Bonn*

64 (below) *The third-century Vimose 'dolphin' baldric.* After Engelhardt 1869

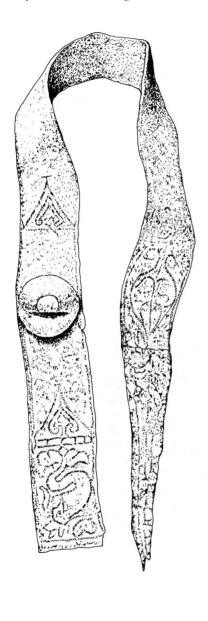

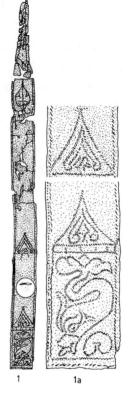

65 (right) *Third-century baldrics from Vimose (1, 1a, 3, 3a, 3b) and Thorsbjerg (2).* After Stjernquist 1954

From the fourth century onwards the dolphin scabbard slide disappears and the waisted type, as typified by the examples on the statue of the Tetrarchs, the Diptych of Stilicho and, in more plebeian terms, on a soldier on a fifth-century Italian plaque showing the 'Life of St Paul', becomes the standard type of scabbard slide. Gone too is the broad baldric with its *phalera* and ivy-leaf terminal fittings. In its place we see the return of both the narrow baldric (as shown on the Diptych of Honorius) and the narrow sword belt (see for example the Diptych of Stilicho).

In the early Byzantine period the scabbard slide method was to some extent replaced by the Avar style 'P' shaped sword suspension system. Used either singly, as in the case of Grave 68 at Visznek, or more commonly in pairs, as is the case with finds from amongst other places Kiszombor and Deszk, they were designed to suspend the sword at an angle from a waist belt.

As to the effectiveness of the sword as a weapon, although Tacitus (*Annals* I.xxxv) appears to show that some swords were sharper than others, both Livy (XXXI.34) and Ammianus (XXXI.7.13-14) paint a picture of a weapon which could easily dismember a body. Against an armoured

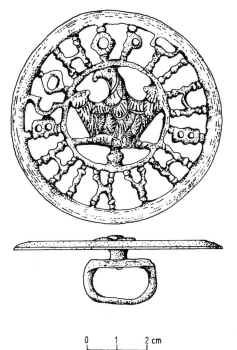

66 (left) *The third-century Carlisle eagle* phalera. After Allason-Jones 1985)

67 (above) *The third-century suckling Romulus and Remus* phalera, *from Egypt*

0   1   2 cm

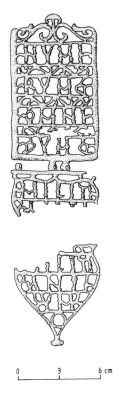

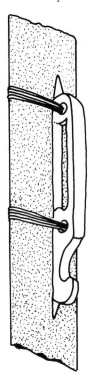

69 *A reconstruction showing how a bone scabbard-slide (the example shown is from London) was attached.* After Chapman 1976

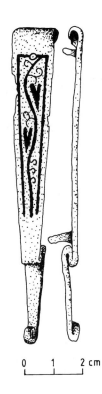

68 *Third-century baldric plates from Zugmantel.* After Oldenstein 1976

70 *A niello decorated iron scabbard-slide from Vimose.* After Hundt 1959/60

opponent the effectiveness of the sword is harder to gauge, although it is highly probable that a heavy enough blow would penetrate the armour. Certainly later thirteenth-century manuscript illustrations show similar weapons to the spatha penetrating helmets (see for example the Maciejowski Bible) and mail (as is shown in the Lansdowne Manuscript).

Finally, what has been viewed as a bit of an oddity, must be considered. The sword in question is 1.8m in length, double-edged, with a narrow pointed blade, a guard, a long grip, but no pommel (**48**). It dates to the late-sixth or early-seventh century AD and was found in the ruins of Byzantine Aphrodisias. It has of course, due to its length, been viewed as symbolic. However, swords almost as large appear in both Sassanian and the Islamic depictions of combat, and similar extremely long 'saddle swords' were carried as a thrusting weapon by Polish cavalrymen as late as the seventeenth century.

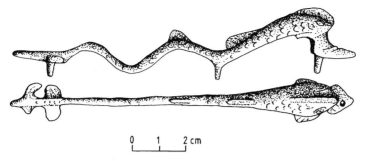

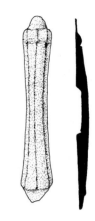

71 *A third-century copper-alloy scabbard-slide from Jagsthausen.*
After Koch 1971)

73 *The Avar sword from Visznek. Note the single 'P' shaped suspension loop.* After Garam et. al. 1975

72 *A Dominate period, wasted bone scabbard-slide from Worms.* After Oldenstein 1976

74 *Short swords, possibly Vegetius' semispathia, from Künzing.* After Herrmann 1969

The military dagger

Had not Agricola been everywhere and ordered his strong, light-armed cohorts to scour the woods, like a cordon, and where the woods were thicker, dismounted cavalry, where thinner, mounted cavalry to do the same, undue confidence might have provoked a serious reverse.

Tacitus, *Agricola*, 37

The dagger in one form or another was a common piece of cavalry equipment throughout the whole of the period under this study. It is harder to say whether or not the dagger was a standard piece of equipment issued to all cavalrymen. However, given the fact that Roman cavalryman was expected to be versatile and fight on both horseback and foot it seems likely that the greater part of the cavalry were equipped with a dagger.

Adopted in the Republican Period from a native Spanish model the *pugio* was used by the Roman cavalry in the first to third centuries AD (**75**). In general terms the *pugio* was a large iron dagger with a blade length of 9-14in. Second- and third-century examples tend to be larger than first-century examples, although this is a general rather than an absolute rule. In specific towns five different blade and two different tang types are identifiable.

Blade Types:

A – Broad waisted blade with a simple mid-rib. (Hod Hill)

B – Heavily waisted blade with a long tapering point, deep grooves either side of the mid-rib. (Vindonissa)

C – Narrow practically straight-edged tapering triangular blade. (Kingsholm)

D – Waisted blade, no mid-ribs or grooves. (Stillfried)

E – Parallel edged blade with grooves either side of the mid-rib (Künzing)

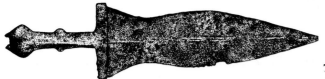

75 *A third-century military dagger from Künzing*

In chronological terms types A–C were in use from the first century AD, type D appeared in the second century AD and type E in the third century AD. Of the tang forms, Type 1 were flat and the hilt was riveted to the blade and the tang. The hilt itself was an inverted 'T' shape with one swelling half-way along the grip and a second at the end acting as a pommel. The hilt was in two halves and sandwiched a layer of bone on horn on either side of the tang.

The second type of tang, the rod tang had the same type of compact hilt as the flat tanged examples save that the rivets holding the hilt together did not pass through the blade or the tang. Instead the end of the tang passed through the pommel and was hammered out – thus holding the hilt in place. In a large number of cases military daggers with rod tangs have been found either without a hilt or with a one-piece carved wooden replacement.

In terms of a blade to tang correlation, although one is discernible in the first century AD; with type A blades having a flat tang, type B blades have both types and type C blades having rod tangs; this neat picture breaks down in the second century.

Sheathes in the first century AD tended to be decorated and to be either frame sheathes, of which plain second and third-century examples are also known. Alternatively they were made from two iron plates, which were joined at the edges, encasing a wooden sheath. Finally, they could have consisted of a leather or wooden sheath with a decorated iron plate attached to its front. The decoration, in all cases, was executed using either inlayed metal (brass, silver, niello) on enamel or metal wires, and took the from of geometric patterns, double-headed axes, temples, garlands, rosettes and palm fronds. Surviving Antonine period and third-century sheathes are all extremely plain. However, as Septimius Severus (Herodian, II.13.10) stripped the Praetorian Guard of their silver and gold inlaid daggers, it is highly possible that highly decorative examples continued in use through until the Dominate when the *pugio* ceased to be used.

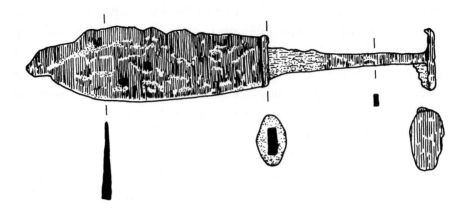

76 *A Dominate period dagger from the Lankhills cemetery.* After Clarke 1979

The dagger was usually suspended vertically and worn on the opposite side to the sword. Although a centurion of the *legio Martia* was depicted wearing his *pugio* horizontally across his stomach. Sheaths were fitted with four suspension rings – this fashion continued into the third century – which allowed the dagger to be suspended either from a waist belt or baldric depending upon individual preference.

Vegetius in the *Epitoma Rei Militaris* (II.15) arms his soldiers with: 'large swords called *spathae*, and other smaller swords called *semispathia*.' No definitively identifiable examples of the *semispathia* exist, however, short swords from the Künzing iron hoards and from Augst, Switzerland, may be examples of this weapon (**74**).

The Künzing and Augst finds both date to the third century. The Künzing find, which contains the most examples, consists of fourteen short swords, which it must be stressed are different to and not to be confused with the Mainz and Pompeii '*gladius*' type legionary swords of the early Empire. The Künzing *semispathia*(?) were pattern-welded and had blade lengths of between 9-16 inches, blade shape varied from parallel, slightly tapering, to fully triangular. Neither hilts nor scabbards have survived, but it is probable that both were of the same design and materials as those used for the *spatha* of the period. Chronologically *semispathia* seem to have been limited to the third and fourth centuries AD. The fourth century saw a radical change in the style and type of dagger used by military, for although the *semispathia* continued in use the *pugio* fell out of favour with the army and was replaced by a range of different weapons.

Although the *pugio* ceased to be used in the late Empire a variant did continue in Spain, the original home of the weapon. These 'Spanish' or as they have also been labelled 'Hispanic-Visigothic' daggers were single edged, with a 6 inch long blade, both the hilt and blade were iron. The knife was carried in a copper-alloy openwork sheath, which was suspended from the waist belt using a ring suspension method – there was a single ring on each side of the scabbard (**77**).

Far more common was a single edged knife, of which the example found in grave 37 at Lankhills is extremely typical. Based, probably upon a Germanic style – numerous examples have been found in the great bog deposits of Ejsbøl I and Illerup - such knives had a blade 5–6 inches in length and a wooden handle. It is likely, as none have been found, that they were carried in a simple leather sheath (**76**).

Viewed as Hunnic in origin, short single-edged swords with single 'P' shaped sword suspension are known from sixth-seventh century AD Sassanian (Iranian/Transoxian) and Ostrogothic/Lombardic (i.e. Nocera Umbra) contexts. Similar weapons have also been found at both Byzantine (i.e. Kerak) and Avar (i.e. Kunpeser) sites.

A Sassanian example in the Metropolitan Museum, New York, has a silver hilt and sheath. Other examples had predominately organic hilts and sheaths, although one of the Kerak finds had a copper-alloy guard and some

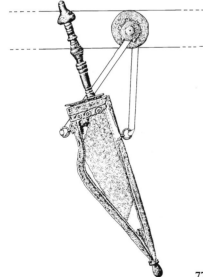

77 *A 'Hispano-Visigothic' dagger.* After Fernández 1996

93

of the Nocera Umbra examples had chapes and pommels. These weapons appear to have been suspended from the waist belt and worn either on the right hip or horizontally across the stomach.

The axe

*The axe crashed down on his head and split it down to the
jaw-bone, spilling the black-teeth onto the ice.*

Njal's Saga, 92

The axe, in a Roman context, is usually seen as a tool and certainly not as a weapon, let alone a cavalry weapon. Yet in the fourth century AD or possibly the third century AD, the axe was adopted as a cavalry weapon by the Roman army. The reasons behind the adoption can only be guessed at, however, a degree of Germanic influence can be perceived as axes similar to those used by the Romans have been found in the bog deposits of Vimose, Thorsbjerg, and Nydam. Nor should its use as a cavalry weapon be seen as strange, for it had been used in this capacity by other cultures since at least the sixth century BC – and it is indeed quite a common find in Scythian burials.

As to the type of axe used, a cavalry-man on a Dominate period tombstone from Gamzigrad, Yugoslavia (**78**), appears to be holding an axe-hammer which is similar in form to a sixth-century find from Butrint, Albania (**80**). However, an extant fourth century AD example from Constantinople Istanbul is more reminiscent of the earlier legionary *dolabra* or pickaxe (**79**).

Avar influence in the Byzantine Period reinforced the use of the axe-hammer as a cavalry weapon, axe-hammers being a common find in Avar weapons graves. However, our understanding of axe suspension is, to say the least, problematic. For despite the fact that the axe was used as a cavalry weapon in Europe up to the mid-seventeenth century there is actually very little evidence for how it was carried.

A complete set of field armour for man and horse in Augsburg, c.1526 by Colman Helmschmid for the future Holy Roman Emperor Ferdinand

78 *A Dominate period tombstone from Gamzigrad. Note the riders axe.* After Bishop & Coulston 1993

I, has an axe suspended by a leather strap from the front, left-hand side of the saddle. The blade of the axe points towards the rider's leg and the strap itself goes around the axe shaft directly below the axe-head.

Alternatively, instead of a simple leather strap, it is possible that the axe shaft was held by an iron ring. In the majority of Avar axe graves an iron ring is also found, the internal diameter of the ring being large enough to accommodate the shaft of the axe, it is thus possible that the ring was hung from the saddle and that this was used to hold the axe (**81**).

A seventh-century gilded silver bowl from Kulagysh/Sassanian Khurasan, currently in the Hermitage, St Petersburg, shows two warriors engaged in combat, at their feet lies an array of broken weapons – including a pair of maces.

Evidence for the use of the mace by the Roman army before the tenth century AD is remarkably slight. The Emperor Maurice's bodyguards were, according to Theophylact Simocatta (VIII.4.13), armed with iron maces. The mace is also included in a sixth century AD Sassanian list of heavy-cavalry equipment, and given the fact that the Roman *cataphracti/clibanarii* were to a large extent based upon the Persian/Sassanian model it seems likely that the mace was introduced into the Roman world from this quarter (**colour plate 16**).

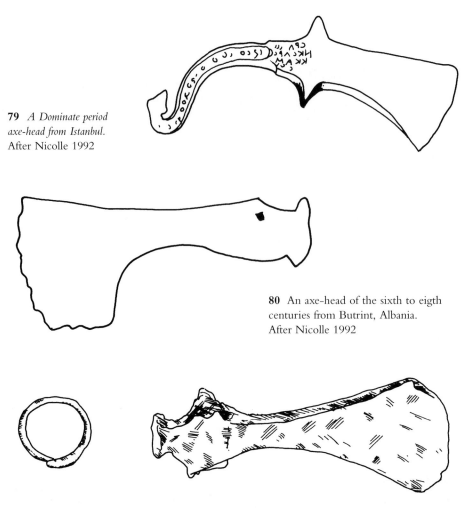

79 *A Dominate period axe-head from Istanbul.* After Nicolle 1992

80 An axe-head of the sixth to eigth centuries from Butrint, Albania. After Nicolle 1992

81 An Avar axe-hammer from Szebény. The ring may have been used to help suspend the axe from a saddle. After Garam et. al. 1975

The axe-hammer and the mace, although effective against the unar-moured, are percussive weapons designed to crush armoured opponents. It is thus likely that their use was in the main confined to the Danubian and Eastern frontiers.

⊰ 9 ⊱

MISSILE WEAPONS

A hit, a very palpable hit.

Shakespeare, *Hamlet*, act V, scene II

Some units, such as the *sagittarii* and the *equites Mauri*, were primarily missile armed. In the cases mentioned above it was the arrow and the javelin respectively. For the rest of the cavalry, with the possible exception of the *contarii*, who may have lacked a missile capability, versatility was the order of the day. The cavalryman was expected to engage the enemy at close quarters with spear and sword, and at a distance with some sort of missile weapon.

The javelin was the main missile weapon for the majority of Roman cavalrymen, although some may have been armed with both javelin and sling. Units of *cataphracti*, *clibanarii*, and possibly *contarii*, were, however, armed after the eastern fashion – their missile weapon being the composite bow. Units of *dromedarii* (camel troops) were armed with both javelin and composite bow.

The javelin

The javelin was basically a smaller version of the spear, albeit without a butt-spike. Josephus (*Jewish War*, III.96) states that they had 'broad points and [were] as long as spears'. However, Polybius and Vegetius are probably more accurate in their descriptions of a smaller weapon.

According to Polybius (VI.22) 'the wooden shaft of the javelin measures about two cubits in length and is about a finger's breadth in thickness; its head is a span long.' Vegetius (*Epitome Rei Militaris*, II.15) describes a very similar weapon, his javelin had 'an iron tip 5in long and a shaft of 3.5ft.' (**82**)

The weapon itself was carried, point down, in a quiver which was hung, for ease of use, on the right-hand side of the horse just behind the rider. As to how many javelins were carried, Josephus (*Jewish War*, III.96) tells us that the Roman cavalryman carried 'three or more'. The 'three' probably represented standard issue, the 'or more' probably represented the reality of campaign and frontier life. It can, however, be said with a fair degree of certainty that of those cavalrymen, whose primary weapon was the javelin, they undoubtedly carried more than three javelins.

The effective range of the javelin, against an unarmoured opponent was approximately 30 yards (27m). At that range it could, if thrown accurately, transfix a human torso. The javelin's armour piercing capabilities increased as the range decreased.

In terms of accuracy, Arrian, in his *Ars Tactica*, paints a picture of great skill and accuracy, albeit in the context of a parade ground display. The *Hippika Gymnasia* should not, however, be viewed simply as dressage under arms. These were serious battlefield manoeuvres that were being practised. Battlefield accuracy is harder to gauge, although the third-century AD writer Julius Africanus (*Kestoi*, 1.1.80-81) claimed that the Roman army was able to achieve one kill for every ten javelins thrown.

During the Dominate and into the early Byzantine period increasing steppe and eastern influence (the Huns, Alans, Avars and Sassanid Persians) led to the displacement of the javelin and the rise of the composite bow as

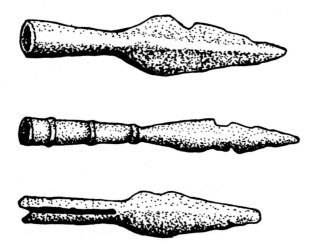

82 *Javelin heads from the Saalburg. After Jacobi 1897*

the standard cavalry missile weapon. It is, however, unlikely that the javelin completely disappeared from the cavalryman's repertoire, particularly in the Western Empire where there was no real tradition of bow-armed cavalry. Javelins are also found, albeit rarely, in Avar graves, although with one possible exception, the associated finds make it impossible to say for certain if they were used by infantry or cavalry. The exception being a late Avar grave at Terehegy, which contained a horse harness and a small spearhead, which might have been a javelin.

The sling

You [cohors VI Commagenorum] *hurled stones from slings.*

From Hadrian's *Adlocutio*, Lambaesis, Africa, AD 128

Although the sling is not normally seen as a cavalry weapon, here we have the emperor Hadrian (AD 117-38) praising its use by cavalrymen from a unit of *equitata*.

It is not known if the cavalrymen of *cohors VI Commagenorum* were mounted or on foot whilst using the sling. Both are possible, albeit with the caveat that if mounted, then they would have been stationary. The sling it must be remembered is not a bolas, which can be used while the horse is in motion.

As to the actual weapon itself, a mid- to late second-century AD sling pouch from Vindolanda, Great Britain, measured 10cm in length. The Vindolanda example was made from thick cattle-hide and decorated with geometric patterning. The weapon was thus not large and combined with a bag of shot (lead, stone or baked-clay) can hardly be seen as an encumbrance for a cavalryman.

In terms of range, estimates of between 150-400m exist, with Vegetius (*Epitome Rei Militaris*, II.23) claiming that a soldier should, with practice, be able to hit a target 180m away. Certainly if only the lower end of the range were actually possible under battlefield conditions then this still gave the average cavalryman a missile weapon which far out ranged the javelin. In terms of the sling's effectiveness, its invisibility in flight and its concussive effect, gave it the ability to incapacitate and even kill armoured opponents.

Leading Vegetius (*Epitome Rei Militaris*, I.16) to write that it was 'more dangerous than any arrows'.

It is impossible to say from this one reference, Hadrian's *Adlocutio*, how far the use of the sling permeated Roman cavalry units. It would certainly have been a useful skill to acquire. However, its inability to be used while the cavalryman was in motion undoubtedly meant that it would remain secondary to the javelin and for that matter the bow, in terms of the cavalryman's missile capability.

The bow

> *Bows suited to the strength of each man, and not above it, more in fact on the weaker side, cases broad enough so that when necessary they can fit the strung bows in them, with spare strings in their saddle bags; quivers with covers holding about thirty or forty arrows.*

> Maurice, *Strategikon*, I.2

The Roman army from the early days of the Empire employed specialist units of horse archers (*sagittarii*) (**91**). Units of *sagittarii* also survived Constantine's reform of the army in the early fourth century AD. However, increasing steppe nomad, the Huns and the Avars, influence in the fifth and sixth centuries led to a de-specialization until by the reign of the emperor Maurice (AD 582-602) the bow, or rather the arrow, had replaced the javelin and become the standard missile weapon of the Roman cavalryman.

Throughout the whole of the period under discussion the composite bow, so called because it was made from wood, sinew and horn or bone, was the war bow of the Roman army (**83** & **84**). No complete examples survive, however, finds of ear- and grip-laths on military sites throughout the empire (see for example the finds from Caerleon, Great Britain) (**85**), coupled with representations of the composite bow on mosaics, sculpture and graffiti (see for example 'Triclinos' hunt mosaic, Apamea, Syria; the tombstone of Flavius Proclus, Mainz, Germany, and one of the Dura grafitti; respectively), all combine to support the argument that the composite bow was the standard war bow of the Roman army from the first

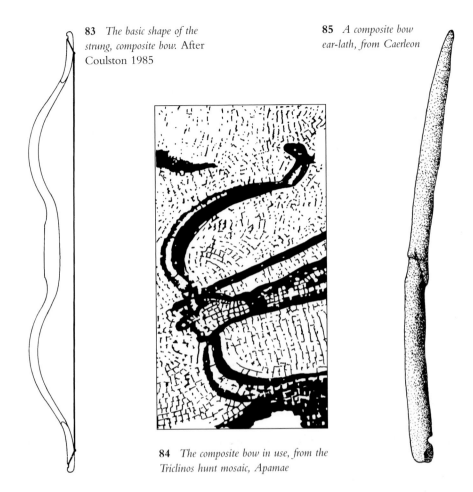

83 *The basic shape of the strung, composite bow.* After Coulston 1985

85 *A composite bow ear-lath, from Caerleon*

84 *The composite bow in use, from the Triclinos hunt mosaic, Apamae*

to the seventh century AD. Vegetius (*Epitome Rei Militaris*, I.14) states that self-bows were used, but purely as training weapons and there is no evidence that they were ever used on the battlefield.

In the main two types of arrowhead were used, armour piercing and anti-personnel. A third, albeit rarer type, incendiary, appears in the archaeological record in the Antonine period. This third type was, however, more probably an infantry as opposed to a cavalry weapon.

The armour piercing arrows had either tanged round (i.e. Carnuntum) and tanged square (i.e. Vindonissa) or socketed square (i.e. Vindonissa) sectioned arrowheads. Anti-personnel arrowheads, however, exhibited a far greater variety of forms. Socketed heads were either angular (i.e. Gundremmingen), single- or double-barbed (i.e. Vindonissa and Szob) in shape. Also from the third century onwards, triple- and quadruple-vaned

101

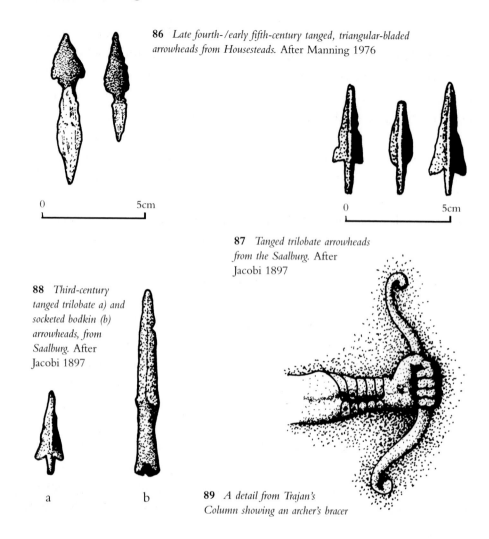

86 *Late fourth-/early fifth-century tanged, triangular-bladed arrowheads from Housesteads.* After Manning 1976

0   5cm

0   5cm

87 *Tanged trilobate arrowheads from the Saalburg.* After Jacobi 1897

88 *Third-century tanged trilobate a) and socketed bodkin (b) arrowheads, from Saalburg.* After Jacobi 1897

a   b

89 *A detail from Trajan's Column showing an archer's bracer*

(i.e. Corbridge) varieties appear. Whilst tanged anti-personnel arrowheads were either trilobate (i.e. Szob and Burnswark) or angular (i.e. Housesteads) in form (**86, 87** & **88**).

As to the arrow shafts (*stele*) themselves, they were made from either wood, or a combination of wood and reed or wood and cane. Where reed or cane was used, then the arrowhead was first attached to a wooden pile, this pile was then glued onto the reed or cane which formed the main body of the shaft. The wooden pile was used in order to reduce the risk of the reed/cane shaft splitting on impact. Splitting, if it occurred, seriously reduced the arrow's penetrative power.

The representational evidence, such as the depiction of an archer's bracer on Trajan's Column and the tombstone of Flavius Proclus, Mainz, show that the 'Mediterranean' release (where the fingers are used to draw the bowstring) was employed by the Roman army (**89 & 90**). However, the archaeological evidence, specifically the *stele* from Dura Europos, a thumbstall from Vindolanda and a thumb-ring currently held in the archery museum at Crépy en Valois, France, also points to the use of 'Mongolian' release (where the thumb was used to draw the bowstring) by the Roman army.

Evidence for the form of the quiver and the bow-case is limited. No examples survive and the evidence is in the main confined to the represent-ational sources.

From the first to the fourth or fifth century AD a cylindrical quiver, suspended from the saddle was used, see for example the tombstone of Flavius Proclus, Mainz. However, steppe influence in the fourth and fifth centuries, led to the adoption of the 'hour-glass' or box-type of quiver. The fourth and fifth centuries also saw a change in the way that the quiver was carried. From this period onwards it was no longer suspended from the saddle, instead it was carried by the rider and hung, steppe fashion, on his right-hand side from a waist belt.

Palmyrene sculpture, such as the relief of 'Asadu and Sa'dai' in the National Museum of Damascus, provides the best evidence for possible the form and location of the bow-case, up until the fourth and fifth centuries AD. Palmyrene bow-cases were roughly trapezoidal in shape and were hung from the right-hand side of the saddle next to the quiver. In some cases the bow-case and quiver were combined. In all cases the bow-case does not appear to have been designed to hold a strung bow (**colour plate 10**).

As with the quiver the bow-case succumbed to steppe influence in the fourth and fifth centuries. In this period the bow-case ceased to be suspended from the saddle, and was carried by the rider, probably on the same belt as the quiver, albeit on the rider's left-hand side. Bow-cases also became 'broad enough so that when necessary they can fit the strung bows in them' (Maurice, *Strategikon*, I.2).

As to the range of the weapon, both the maximum and effective ranges need to be considered, yet neither can be given with any certainty. Therefore, before looking at the range of the bow, the first thing to do is to consider the reasons behind this uncertainty.

90 *The first-century AD tombstone of Flavius Proclus, Mainz*

Range was as much dependent upon the man as the bow. The draw weight of the bow needed to be tailored to the strength of the user. Indeed as the Emperor Maurice points out in his *Strategikon* (I.2), the 'bow [should be] suited to the strength of each man, and not above it, more in fact on the weaker side.' While the anonymous *Byzantine Treatise on Strategy* (44) recommended drawing the bowstring to the ear, as this produced the most powerful shot, it also states that the bowstring could be drawn to the neck or the breast. Coupled with this was bow quality, the better made the composite bow the better the performance. In addition infantry bows were larger and more powerful than cavalry bows. All of these factors influenced the performance of the weapon and are the reasons behind the uncertainties and debate over the actual range of the composite bow.

Vegetius (*Epitome Rei Militaris*, II.23) tells us that archers 'used to put up scopae, i.e. bundles of brushwood or straw, for a target, removing themselves 600ft from the target, to practise hitting it frequently with arrows'. The sixth-century anonymous *Byzantine Treatise on Strategy* (47), however, recommends shooting at targets which are approximately 56m from the archer. In later Islamic sources, skilled archers were expected to hit a one metre wide target from a distance of 69-75m, although the range of their composite bow was seen as being between 300-400 cubits (or approximately 180-240m). Modern research tends to place effective range at between 50-150m.

91 *Graffito of a horse-archer from Dura Europos.* After Mielczarek 1993

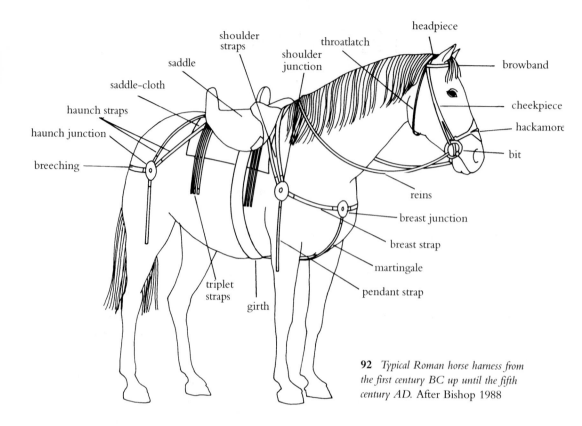

shoulder
straps

saddle

saddle-cloth

haunch straps

haunch junction

breeching

triplet
straps

girth

shoulder
junction

throatlatch

headpiece

browband

cheekpiece

hackamore

bit

reins

breast junction

breast strap

martingale

pendant strap

92 *Typical Roman horse harness from the first century BC up until the fifth century AD.* After Bishop 1988

Maximum range has been calculated as being between approximately 165-230m. The calculation of maximum range appears at first sight to be a pointless task, for beyond effective range the archer would be fortunate to inflict serious damage upon an opponent. However, this is to take a limited view of the bow's potential. For actions such as Agincourt (AD 1415) show that the bow had the ability, even beyond effective range, to adversely affect the enemy's morale and to precipitate a fatally ill-considered response.

⊰ 10 ⊱

THE SADDLE

What can be said about the saddle? Firstly it is not strictly speaking a piece of military equipment, yet it does to some extent dictate the fighting capabilities of the cavalryman, although this point can be and indeed has been overstated (**92** & **97**).

At some point in the first century BC the Roman army adopted the four-horned saddle from the Celts. The cavalryman's horse on the first century BC Altar of Domitius Ahenobarbus lacks a saddle; however, the horses on the Tiberian (AD 14-37) Arch at Orange are equipped with the four-horned saddle.

The saddle consisted of a wooden frame, or tree. Attached to the frame's wooden horns were copper-alloy horn plates, of which the Newstead, Scotland, examples are probably the most famous. The function of these plates is uncertain, they may have been used to protect or strengthen the wooden horns, alternatively they could have been used as shapers for the horns. The frame was also padded and covered with a leather saddle cover, examples of which survive from Vindolanda, England, and Valkenburg, Netherlands (**93**, **94**, **95** & **96**).

The four-horned saddle continued in use until in the early fifth century AD it was replaced by the steppe saddle (**99**). The steppe saddle, of which the earliest possible illustration in a Roman context occurs in the early fifth century AD Vatican Vergil (Vat. Lat. 3225, Folio 63r), is to modern eyes a more recognizable saddle. As with the four-horned saddle a wooden frame was employed, however, the steppe saddle had in the main, a raised pommel at the front and a cantle at the back. An exception to this rule can be seen on a seventh-century Byzantine Armenian carving in Mrèn Cathedral, Armenia, here the saddle has a raised pommel, but it lacks a cantle.

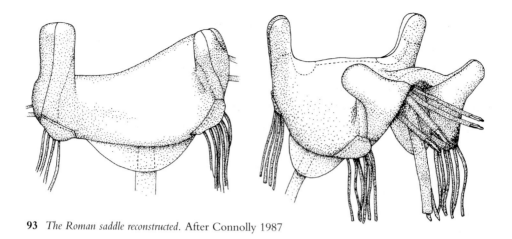

93 *The Roman saddle reconstructed.* After Connolly 1987

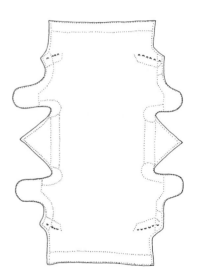

94 *A reconstruction of the underside of the Roman saddle.* After Connolly 1987

95 *A reconstruction of the Valkenburg leather saddle cover.* After Groenman-van Waateringe 1967

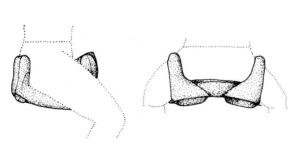

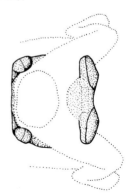

97 *These illustrations show how secure a seat was provided by the Roman four-horned saddle.* After Connolly 1987

An unusual style of saddle was depicted on the now lost Diocletianic military frescos from the dynastic temple complex at Luxor (**98**). Copies of the fresco illustrations do survive, however, due to their unique nature it is only possible to speculate on the construction of the saddles. The Luxor saddles appear to have had a quilted, padded cover and they were possibly wooden framed with (as some reconstructions suggest) a low pommel and cantle.

The stirrup was introduced into west by the Avars in the sixth or early seventh century (**100**). The speed of its adoption by the Byzantine army is unknown, however, the fact that it is listed as a standard piece of equipment in the *Strategikon* (I.2) of Maurice, as well as being depicted in Byzantine Armenian art (see for example the carving in the church in Ptghni, Armenia), does suggest that it rapidly became commonplace.

The horse was not the only beast of burden employed by the Roman army, the camel was also used. Its use was initially confined to that of pack animal. The camel became a cavalry mount when the Emperor Trajan (AD 98-117) created the *ala I Ulpia Dromedariorum Milliaria Palmyrenorum* (**colour plate 10**).

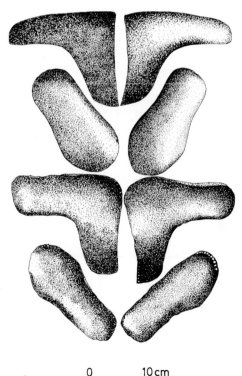

96 *The copper-alloy saddle-horn plates from Newstead*

0   10 cm

98 The Dominate period saddle from the Imperial Chamber at Luxor

99 The Avar saddle, note the stirrups. This replaced the four-horned saddle in the fifth century AD. After Nicolle 1990

100 An early-Avar stirrup from Dévaványa. After Garam et. al. 1975

The dromedary saddle consisted of a padded, quilted cloth, which covered the top of the body. Over this was placed a wooden frame, which was arched at the front and back. Between the two arches was a second padded, quilted cloth on which the rider sat.

Throughout the whole of the Imperial period the Roman cavalryman, be he on horse or camel, was provided with a secure seat from which to fight. The lack of stirrups for most of the period under study is neither here nor there. The importance of the stirrup has been over-emphasized, as the Roman cavalryman was perfectly able to engage in shock combat with spear and sword without them. Indeed it has been asserted that the main initial impact of the stirrup was to reduce fatigue on long distance rides.

⊰ 11 ⊱

HORSE ARMOUR

*Since the rider is seriously imperilled in the event of his horse being wounded,
the horse should also be armed, having head, chest and thigh pieces: the last
also serve to cover the rider's thighs. But above all the horse's belly must be
protected; for this, which is the most vital part, is also the weakest.*

Xenophon, *On The Art of Horsemanship*, XII.8

Horse armour, with the possible exception of the chamfron, does not seem
to have been in general use by the Roman Cavalry, although its use appears
to have increased in the early Byzantium Period. In the main horse armour
appears to have been confined to units of heavily armoured *cataphracti* and
clibanarii (**101**); *contarii* although similarly armed seem to have ridden unar-
moured horses.

Six types of horse armour are discernible from the sources; chamfrons
for the head, crinets for the neck, peytrals for the chest, trappers for the
body, knemides for the legs, and iron plates for the hooves.

Chamfrons

From the first to the third century a number of different types of chamfron
are discernible archaeologically. However, from the Dominate onwards the
evidence becomes purely literary and representational.

Chamfrons, in the pre-Dominate period, fall into two main types; the
first type covered the front and side of the horse's head, while the second
protected only the eyes. Of the first type both leather and metal varieties

111

101 *The graffito of the* cataphracti/clibanarii *from Dura Europos.* After Mielczarek 1993

exist. A first to second century AD example from Vindolanda, Great Britain, typifies the leather type. Vindolanda Chamfron I was made from 4-5mm thick cowhide, it would have covered the face of the horse, and had two flaps for the ears. Although it had two circular eyeholes, the chamfron did not protect the horse's eyes in any way. It is possible that metal eye-guards were originally attached to the chamfron, however, despite the fact the chamfron is damaged around the eyeholes there is no real evidence to either support of refute the use of metal eye-guards. The chamfron was decorated with metal studs (**102**).

The metal full-face chamfrons are typified by a number of third-century examples from Gherla, Romania, and Strasbourg, Germany. The Gherla and Strasbourg finds consisted of a number of copper-alloy triple chamfron plates, which covered the front and side of the horse's head. Unlike the leather chamfron they lacked earflaps, but had eye-guards. They were decorated in raised relief with images of Dioscuri, Mars, Minerva, Victory, snakes, eagles, dolphins, lions, phalera and tombs (**colour plates 11 & 14**).

Of the second type, which only protected the eyes. These could be very simple, no more than open-work metal domes with strap attachments. See for example a number of examples which were found in the Rhine near Mainz; or they consisted of a highly decorated hexagonal centre plate to which was attached two (again highly decorated) tear-drop shaped eye-guards. The examples from Strasbourg are decorated in the same way as their larger counterparts.

From the fourth century onwards there is a lack of evidence for the second style of chamfron, although descriptions of *cataphracti* and *clibanarii* show that the chamfron continued in use in this period. In the early Byzantine period chamfrons which covered the face and side of the horse's head continued in use, however, along side the probable continence of both copper-alloy and leather examples, iron and lamellar chamfrons were also used; see for example Maurice's *Strategikon* (I.2) and the contemporaneous seventh century AD Sassanian relief at Taq-i Bustan, Iran.

As to their use, the introduction of the chamfron pre-dated the raising of units of heavy cavalry (*cataphracti* and *clibanarii*) by the Roman Army. It is thus likely that up until, certainly the end of the third century AD that chamfrons were, or rather could be, used by all cavalry regiments regardless of type. From the Dominate onwards, although they continued to be used by heavy cavalry and also possibly medium cavalry, it is very probable that their use was discontinued by those units which fulfilled a light cavalry role.

102 *The leather chamfron from Vindolanda.* After van Driel–Murray 1989

0   10   20 cm

113

The crinet

Included amongst the mid–third century AD artefacts found at Dura Europos, Syria, were two large, albeit incomplete, sections of lamellar armour. They were made from rawhide, in one case coloured red and in the other black, in both cases the lamellae and are approximately 7cm long by 4.5cm wide. The lamellae are laced together using red leather laces. The red section of lamellar armour was 77cm long, and had an upper width of 60cm and a lower width of 27cm; the black example was 61cm long, with an upper width of 48cm and a lower of 21cm (**colour plates 11 & 14**).

They are usually identified as thigh-guards or 'armoured cowboy chaps'. They are, however, too big to be thigh-guards. A more likely explanation is that each piece formed one half of a crinet, and that they protected the horse's neck as opposed to the rider's thighs. Leaving to one side the debate over the identification of the Dura Europos finds; crinets do appear both on the graffiti of the *cataphracti/clibanarii* again for Dura Europos and also on the Taq-i Bustan relief. The later example is presumably lamellar, whilst the former may well show either scale or solid-scale.

Crinet's are also described as being used by Ammianus (XVI.10.8 implicitly, and XXIV.6.8 explicitly) and are recommended, explicitly both by Maurice (*Strategikon* I.2) and by the anonymous *Byzantine Treatise on Strategy* (17).

Peytrals

Peytrals, or chest protectors, appear on the late second century BC Pergamum trophy reliefs, yet despite this early appearance the evidence for

103 *The possible leather peytral from Vindolanda.* After van Driel-Murray 1989

their use in the Imperial Period is limited. Flavian period tombstones, such as those of T. Flavius Bassus and Lucius (both in Koln Museum), depict horses wearing what may be peytrals, but more probably show decorative fringed bands. However, a leather fragment from Vindolanda, Great Britain, may have formed part of a peytral (**103**).

In the early Byzantine period the evidence improves slightly, Maurice in his *Strategikon* (I.2) states that horses should have 'breast plates of iron or felt, or else breast and neck coverings such as the Avars use.'

This Avar style of armour may well have been lamellar and is in all probability represented on an early seventh century AD Sassanian rock carving at Taq-i Bustan, Iran. Here the Sassanian cavalryman's horse wears a peytral of lamellar, the pieces of which (lamellae) overlap forwards and upwards.

The trapper

The body of the horse was protected by a trapper. What are believed to be cloth (felt on quilted) examples appear on the fourth century AD Sassanian reliefs at Naqsh-i Rustam, Iran; while the tenth century *Praecepta militaria* (III. 37-45) of the Emperor Nikephoros II Phokas (AD 963-969) recommends the use:

> . . . *either of pieces of felt and boiled leather fastened together down to the knees so that nothing of the horse's body appears except its eyes and nostrils – likewise their legs below the knees and their undersides should remain uncovered and unconcealed – or they can have klibania made of bison hides over the chest of the horse which should be split at its legs and underneath to permit the unhindered movement of their legs.*

> *Praecepta militaria* III 37-45

It is also likely, given the fact that it was also used for peytrals and crinets, that lamellar was also used for trappers. However, the best evidence for the trapper comes from Dura Europos. The finds, which date to the mid-third century AD consist not only of a graffito of a *cataphractus/clibanarius* whose horse wears a scale trapper, but more importantly of three scale trappers, two of which are complete (**104, colour plates 11 & 14**).

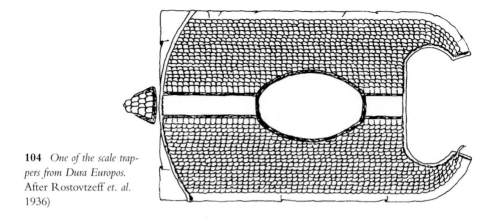

104 *One of the scale trappers from Dura Europos.* After Rostovtzeff *et. al.* 1936)

Housing I had copper-alloy scales (length 35mm, width 25mm) and was 1.22m long and 1.69m wide. The scales, of which there were 31 rows per side, were attached to each other by copper-alloy wire and to the trapper's cloth backing with linen thread. Across the spine there was an oval opening to accommodate the saddle. The spine, the edges of the opening and the lower edges of the trapper were covered with red leather. The base of the tail was protected by a triangular section of scales, which was also edged in red leather. Some of the leather thongs, which attached the trapper to the saddle and horse harness, as well as to a separate scale peytral, survived.

Housing II, which had iron scaled (length 60mm, width 45mm) was 1.48m long and 1.10m wide. The scales, of which there were only 19 rows per side, were attached to the textile backing using leather thong or laces. As with Housing I there was an oval opening for the saddle, the spine was not armoured and there was a triangular section of scales to protect the tail. However, unlike Housing I the horse's chest was protected by the two curving extensions.

The fragmentary trapper was made from copper-alloy scales attached to a textile backing. There is no evidence that any form of under-armour padding was worn with this armour. Indeed such use is highly unlikely for two reasons, firstly, the armour was primarily designed to offer a measure of protection against arrows and glancing blows in the melee; secondly on a practical level, the very real and very debilitating problem of heat exhaustion would have been exacerbated by any such additional layer.

Knemides

Heliodorus, in his late fourth century AD novel, The *Aethiopica* (IX.15.4) claims that the legs of the horses of the Persian cataphracts were protected by '*knemides*'.

The word '*knemides*' has been translated to mean either greaves or quilted leggings. With the possible exception of the all-over scale Sarmatians on Trajan's Column, there is no representational evidence to support the use of '*knemides*'. Indeed it is entirely possible that Heliodorus is exaggerating the amount of armour worn, the *Aethiopica* is after all a novel. Alternatively, and giving Heliodorus the benefit of the doubt, '*knemides*' may have been used to protect the horses legs, but rather than being attached to their legs, they may instead have been long skirted extensions at the front and back of the horses trapper, such as were used by Sudanic heavy cavalry in the nineteenth century AD.

The hooves

> *The horse's hooves should be protected by iron plates, so they will not be injured by caltrops and similar devices.*

> Anonymous, *Byzantine Treatise on Strategy*, (17)

The Anonymous sixth-century *Byzantine Treatise on Strategy* was probably written in the latter part of the reign of Justinian (527–65). The unknown author had a very sound and practical knowledge of field engineering and fortifications and it is most probable that he was a veteran and that he had seen some combat. However, some of the *Treatise* is more theoretical and appears to have been derived from earlier sources. Where then, in this mixture of the practical and theoretical, do these hoof protectors fit? Given the paucity of evidence it is difficult to say, they may have been used at a siege at which the author was present, alternatively they may be a theoretical invention which the author, again possibly based upon personal observation, deem a necessary part of the heavy cavalryman's equipment.

APPENDIX:
DESCRIPTION OF COLOUR RECONSTRUCTIONS

Colour plate 8: An Antonine period horse archer

The rider, in mid-Parthian shot, is employing the Mediterranean release. His conical helmet, solid-scale armour and ring pommel sword, were all first used by the Roman army in the Antonine period. Junction *phalera* with peripheral loops replaced the concealed loop variety in this period.

Colour plate 9: A Flavian cavalryman

Although not normally associated with the early Empire, long sleeved, cuffed tunics do appear on a number of first and second-century cavalry monuments. The body armour, with its shoulder-doubling, is typical of the period. The helmet is copied from the Ely find and the man is armed with long sword and military dagger. However, instead of a spear he has a *lituus* or J-shaped horn. The horse is shown in full Flavian finery, which would have been worn both on parade and in battle. By this period junction *phalera* with concealed loops had replaced free-moving junction loops.

Colour plate 10: A third-century *dromedarius*.

Roman *dromedarii* were based upon Palmyrene troops. The main parts of the equipment were a helmet and body armour, in this case both Roman; a composite bow and a quiver of arrows; a quiver of javelins; long spear; a military dagger; and a long sword, the sword illustrated has a Palmyrene hilt but the sword suspension method is Roman. Instead of a small round Palmyrene shield he carries a standard hexagonal Roman shield. By the third-century long sleeved tunics and long trousers were *de rigueur* for the Roman soldier. The pattern on the trousers is Palmyrene.

Colour plates 11 & 14: A third-century *clibanarius*

Contus and bow armed, after the eastern fashion, *clibanarii* formed the heavy shock cavalry of the Roman army. The horse is protected by a scale trapper, lamellar crinnet (both based upon the finds from Dura Europos) and a hinged triple chamfron. The man has a full-face mask helmet and his neck is protected by a gorget (based upon the atalka find). He also wears a knee length, long sleeved mail shirt over which is placed a solid-scale shirt. His knees and lower legs are protected by greaves. The multiple layers of armour are designed to compensate for the lack of a shield. The whole image, from the unchanging masked face to the bright colours and tall plumes was designed to overawe the enemy.

Colour plate 12: A Dominate light cavalryman

As is the case here, during the Dominate some javelin armed light cavalry discarded their body armour, although they retained the *thoracomachus*. The figure also wears an 'Intercisa' type ridge helmet and carries a broad oval shield with a Germanic shield-boss.

Colour plate 13: A Typical Tiberio-Claudian harness

Prior to the introduction of the steppe saddle in the fifth-century Roman horse harness saw little change. Such change as did occur was confined to the decorative elements and to the actual physical form of the junction fittings. In the early Principate free-moving junction loops were used.

Colour plate 15: A Dominate period cavalry *draconarius*

The silver and gilded snake's head standard is from Niederbieber, Germany, while the eagle-hilted sword is based upon the examples shown on the statue of the Tetrarchs in Venice. The figure's armour is based upon the fragmentary fourth-century relief of two soldiers in the Vatican Museo Chiaramonti. The helmet is Berkasovo No. 1.

Colour plate 16: Early Byzantine horse harness

At some point in the fifth century the steppe saddle replaced the Celtic four-horned saddle. Stirrups are mentioned as a standard piece of cavalry equipment in the *Strategikon* (I.2) of Maurice.

Colour plate 17: Early Byzantine cavalryman 1

Based upon the figure of the cavalryman on the Isola Rizza dish, the figure wears the lamellar helmet and armour found at Niederstotzingen. From a waist-belt worn under the armour an Avar sword is suspended. The axe is also Avar. The very long sword in the figure's right hand was found at Aphrodisias.

Colour plate 18: Early Byzantine cavalryman 2

Based upon Maurice's *Strategikon*, the figure wears a hooded, ankle length coat of mail, with an Avar gorget. The lamellar helmet is from Kertsch. The gauntlets are based upon a sixth- seventh-century Iranian example. He has an Avar ring-pommel sword and his bow/bow-case and quiver are suspended steppe fashion from a waist belt. He has an iron mace in his left hand, while the spear in his right hand is fitted with a leather carrying strap.

SELECT BIBLIOGRAPHY

Abler, T.S. 1999: *Hinterland Warriors and Military Dress: European Empires and Exotic Uniforms*, Oxford.

Allason-Jones, L. & Bishop, M.C. 1988: *Excavations at Roman Corbridge: The Hoard*, London.

Arnold, T. 2001: *The Renaissance at War*, London.

Bar-Kochva, B. 1976: *The Seleucid Army*, Cambridge.

Blackmore, D. 1990: *Arms & Armour of the English Civil Wars*, London.

Bishop, M.C. & Coulston, J.C.N. 1993: *Roman Military Equipment: from the Punic Wars to the fall of Rome*, London.

Born, H. & Junkelmann, M. 1997: *Römische Kampf- und Turnierrüstungen*, Mainz am Rhein.

Boss, R. 1993: *Justinian's Wars: Belisarius, Narses and the Reconquest of the West*, Stockport.

Brzezinski, R. & Mielczarek, M. 2002: *The Sarmatians 600BC-AD450*, Oxford.

Cernenko, E.V. 1983: *The Scythians 700-300BC*, Oxford.

Connolly, P. 1988: *Tiberius Claudius Maximus: The Cavalryman*, Oxford.

Coulston, J.C. 1988: *Military Equipment and the Identity of Roman Soldiers*, Oxford.

Dixon, K.R. & Southern P. 1992: *The Roman Cavalry: From the First to the Third Century AD*, London.

Dodgeon, M.H. & Lieu, S.N.C. (eds.) 1991: *The Roman Eastern Frontier and the Persian Wars AD226-363: A Documentary History*, London.

van Driel-Murray, C. 1989: *Roman Military Equipment: the Sources of Evidence*, Oxford.

Elton, H. 1996: *Warfare in Roman Europe AD350-425*, Oxford.

Feest, C. 1980: *The Art of War*, London.

Feugère, M. 1993: *Les Armes des Romains*, Paris.

Feugère, M. 1994: *Casques Antiques*, Paris.

Garam, E., Kovrig, I., Szabo, J.GY. & Torok, GY. 1975: *Avar Finds in the Hungarian National Museum*, Budapest.

Garbsch, J. 1978: *Romische Paraderustungen*, Munchen.

Greatrex, G. 1998: *Rome and Persia at War, 502-532*, Leeds.

Goldsworthy, A.K. 1996: *The Roman Army at War 100BC-AD200*, Oxford.

Gorelik, M.V. 1995: *Warriors of Eurasia: from the VIII century BC to the XVII century AD*, Stockport.

Haldon, J. 1999: *Warfare, State and Society in the Byzantine World 565-1204*, London.

Haldon, J. 2000: *The Byzantine Wars*, Stroud.

Hanson, V.D. 1999: *The Wars of the Ancient Greeks*, London.

Haythornthwaite, P.J. 2001: *Napoleonic Cavalry*, London.

Hoffmeyer, A.B.de 1972: *Arms and Armour in Spain a short survey vol. I: The Bronze Age to the End of the High Middle Ages*, Madrid.

Hyland, A. 1993: *Training the Roman Cavalry: From Arrian's* Ars Tactica, Stroud.

Junkelmann, M. 1990: *Die Reiter Roms I*, Mainz am Rhein.

Junkelmann, M. 1991: *Die Reiter Roms II*, Mainz am Rhein.

Junkelmann, M. 1992: *Die Reiter Roms III*, Mainz am Rhein.

Junkelmann, M. 1996: *Reiter wie Statuen aus Erz*, Mainz am Rhein.

Junkelmann, M. 2000: *Römische Helme*, Mainz am Rhein.

Kennedy, H. 2001: *The Armies of the Caliphs: Military and Society in the Early Islamic State*, London.

Kennedy, H. 2002: *Mongols, Huns & Vikings*, London.

Kiss, A. 1977: *Avar Cemeteries in County Baranya*, Budapest.

Klumbach, H. (ed.) 1973: *Spätrömische Gardehelme*, Munich.

Klumbach, H. 1974: *Römische Helme aus Niedergermanien*, Cologne.

Lepper, F. & Frere, S. 1988: *Trajan's Column*, Gloucester.

Lev, Y. (ed.) 1997: *War and Society in the Eastern Mediterranean*, Leiden.

McCall, J.B. 2002: *The Cavalry of the Roman Republic: Cavalry combat and elite reputations in the middle and late Republic*, London.

McGreer, E. 1995: *Sowing the Dragon's Teeth: Byzantine Warfare in the Tenth Century*, Washington.

Mielczarek, M. 1993: *Cataphracti and Clibanarii: studies on the heavy armoured cavalry of the ancient world*, Lodz.

Mielczarek, M. 1999: *The Army of the Bosporan Kingdom*, Lodz.

Montagu, J.D. 2000: *Battles of the Greek and Roman Worlds: A chronological compendium of 667 battles to 31BC from the historians of the ancient world*, London.

Nadolski, A. 1974: *Polish Arms: Side-Arms*, Warsaw.

Nicolle, D. 1984: *The Age of Charlemagne*, London.

Nicolle, D. 1990: *Attila and the Nomad Hordes: Warfare on the Eurasian Steppes 4th-12th centuries*, London.

Nicolle, D. 1991: *Rome's Enemies 5: The Desert Frontier*, London.

Nicolle, D. 1992: *Romano-Byzantine Armies 4th-9th centuries*, London.

Nicolle, D. 1993: *Armies of the Muslim Conquest*, Oxford.

Nicolle, D. 1994: *Yarmuk 636AD: The Muslim conquest of Syria*, Oxford.

Nicolle, D. 1995: *Medieval Warfare Source Book Volume 1: Warfare in Western Christendom*, London.

Nicolle, D. 1996: *Medieval Warfare Source Book Volume 2: Christian Europe and its Neighbours*, London.

Nicolle, D. 1996: *Sassanian Armies: The Iranian Empire early 3rd to mid-7th centuries AD*, Stockport.

Nicolle, D. (ed.) 2002: *A Companion to Medieval Arms and Armour*, Woodbridge.

Obmann, J. 2000: *Studien zu römischen Dolchscheiden des 1. Jahrhunderts n. Chr.*, Cologne.

Parker, G. 1996: *The Military Revolution: Military innovation and the rise of the West 1500-1800* (2nd Edition), Cambridge.

Pleiner, R. 1993: *The Celtic Sword*, Oxford.

Rankov, B. 1994: *The Praetorian Guard*, London.

Richmond, I. 1982: *Trajan's Army on Trajan's Column*, London.

Robinson, H.R. 1967: *Oriental Armour*, London.

Robinson, H.R. 1975: *The Armour of Imperial Rome*, London.

Sekunda, N. 1984: *The Army of Alexander the Great*, Oxford.

Sekunda, N. 1994: *Seleucid and Ptolemaic Reformed Armies 168-145BC. Volume 1: The Seleucid Army*, Stockport.

Sekunda, N. 1995: *Seleucid and Ptolemaic Reformed Armies 168-145BC. Volume 2: The Ptolemaic Army*, Stockport.

Sekunda, N. 1996: *Roman Republican Army 200-104BC*, Oxford.

Snodgrass, A.M. 1999: *Arms & Armour of the Greeks* (rev. ed.), Baltimore.

Southern, P. & Dixon, K.R. 1996: *The Late Roman Army*, London.

Spence, I.G. 1993: *The Cavalry of Classical Greece: A Social and Military History with Particular Reference to Athens*, Oxford.

Speidel, M.P. 1994: *Riding for Caesar: The Roman Emperors' Horse Guard*, London.

Spring, C. 1993: *African Arms and Armour*, London.

Stephenson, I.P. 1999: *Roman Infantry Equipment: The Later Empire*, Stroud.

Sumner, G. 1997: *Roman Army Wars of the Empire*, London.

Thomas, E.B. 1971: *Helme Schilde Dolche*, Budapest.

Tincey, J. 2002: *Ironsides: English Cavalry 1588-1688*, Oxford.

Tylden, G. 1965: *Horses and Saddlery*, London.

Webber, C. 2001: *The Thracians 700BC-AD46*, Oxford.

Whitby, M. 1988: *The Emperor Maurice and his Historian: Theophylact Simocatta on Persian and Balkan Warfare*, Oxford.

Wright, D.H. 1993: *The Vatican Vergil: A Masterpiece of Late Antique Art*, Berkeley.

INDEX

Agincourt, battle of, 106
Alans, 98
Altar of Domitius Ahenobarbus, 107
Ammianus, 14-5, 21, 24, 52, 57, 87, 114
Anonymous, *Byzantine Treatise on Strategy*,
   53, 62, 105, 114, 117
Antonine period, 10, 19, 24, 43, 47-8,
   66, 78, 82, 91
Arch at Orange, 17, 107
Arch of Constantine, 34, 39
Arch of Diocletian, 47
Arch of Galerius, 12, 34, 39
Arlon 13, 50
army groups, 12
Arrian, *Ars Tactica*, 21, 98
Augustus, 10, 17
Avar, 14, 31, 49, 68-69, 78-79, 87, 93-5,
   98-9, 115
axe, 75, 94-6, 121
   dolabra, 94
   suspension, 94-5

Battle of Ebenezer fresco, Dura Europos,
   19, 71
bladed weapons, 75-96
blunt trauma, 52
body armour, 43-53
   breastplates, 44-5, 48
   composite, 43, 49-50
   lamellar, 43, 48-9, 114, 120-21
   lorica plumata, 49
   mail, 13, 43-7, 120-21
   padding and effectiveness, 51-53
   scale, 43-7
   segmentata, 50
   shoulder-doubling, 44, 119
   solid-scale, 43, 47-8, 119-120
   splint, 50
bolas, 99
bows, 66, 97, 99, 100-106
   arrows, 101-102
   bow case, 103, 119-20
   bracer, 103
   composite bow, 100, 119-20
   quiver, 103, 119-20

range, 103-106
self bow, 101
thumbstall/thumb-ring, 103
'Buffalo Bill's Wild West', 15
Byzantine, 10, 14, 31, 34, 40, 43-4, 47, 49,
   66, 78-9, 87-8, 93, 98, 107, 113, 115

Caesar, 14, 52
caracole, 15
cataphracti/clibanarii, 14, 42, 50, 55-57, 62-
   3, 95, 97, 111, 113-14, 116
Column of Arcadius, 39
Constantine, 9
Constantius, 14, 57, 63
contarii/contus, 35, 42, 56, 71-3, 97, 111,
   120
Crossing the Red Sea mosaic, S. Maria
   Maggiore, Rome, 24, 27, 34, 47

dagger, 75, 90-94
   Hispano-Visigothic, 12, 93
   Hunnic, 93
   pugio, 90-3
   semispathia, 92
   single edged, 93
De Rebus Bellicis, 52-3, 62
Diocletian, 24
Diptych of Stilicho, 40
Dominate, 10, 14, 43, 47, 91, 93-4, 98,
   111, 113
dromedarii, 35, 97, 109, 120
Dura Europos, 12, 19, 20, 34-36, 39-40,
   42, 45, 48, 50, 55-56, 62, 71, 114, 116

Ejsbøl I, 93

falces, 56
Flavius Proclus, 103

Gaugamela, battle of, 59
gauntlets, 58, 121
Germanic, 14, 34-6, 39-40, 79
Gokstad, 39
gorget, 55, 58-61
   Avar, 59-61, 121

125